CREATIVE CONTAINERS

NANCY GARDINER

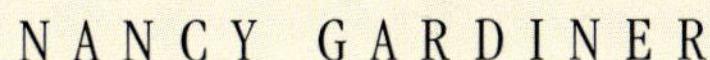

CREATIVE CONTAINERS

A practical and inspirational guide to container gardening in South Africa

METZ PRESS

To my family, with my love

Author's Acknowledgements

Among the many people who have helped to make this book, I would like to give special thanks to Celtiskloof and Dunrobin nurseries for their unfailing willingness to help. Also, to Keith Kirsten, for generously allowing me to take photographs in his garden and nursery. And a very special thank you to Wilsia Metz for her patience and encouragement at all times.

Published by Metz Press
1 Cameronians Avenue
Welgemoed 7530
South Africa

First published in 1996

Editor and coordinator: Wilsia Metz
Copy editor and indexer: Ethné Clarke
Designer: Alix Gracie, T/A Design Dynamix, Cape Town
Illustrator: Kobie Ferreira
Photographs: Nancy Gardiner
Repro coordinator: Andrew de Kock
Reproduction: Positive Image, Cape Town
Printing: Wing King Tong Co. Ltd., Hong Kong

ISBN 1-875001-25-5

Contents

Introduction

In recent years, container gardening has taken on a new dimension, as new and vastly varied containers have become available to suit every taste. From the plain and simple to the ornate and highly decorative, they offer the gardener many new aspects of this fascinating form of gardening. For the townhouse or the large garden, for the balcony garden or the roof garden, containers have many advantages. They can be used to achieve dramatic and colourful results in small spaces, or, in larger gardens, to create focal points, or as links between different parts of the garden. A container is a garden in itself – a garden which, with careful thought and planning, can be beautiful all through the changing of the seasons. Because of the relatively small size of a container its soil can be replenished or replaced regularly and with ease, ready for the next batch of plants. Provided that they are not too heavy, containers can be moved to those parts of the garden where they will make a greater impact, or it may be necessary to move container-grown plants away from a spot where the shade is too heavy or the sunlight too bright.

Container-grown plants may be permanent or temporary. A single calamondin (miniature citrus) in a pretty pot will bring great pleasure in winter with its harvest of small, brightly coloured fruits, and even in summer its foliage is attractive. At the other end of the scale, a tub or pot filled to overflowing with bright and happy spring annuals will be a joy. And when their flowering season is over, the colours of summer will take their place. Virtually anything can be grown in containers, provided they are given the right conditions of soil, light, warmth, water and food. Knowing and fulfilling the needs of your container-grown plants will bring a great sense of satisfaction as they burgeon under your care.

Containers have a place in almost any part of the garden – from the patio, front door and steps, to the far-flung parts where there may be a lack of interest. They should be an inherent part of the garden design – to create a contrast or a blending of colours and textures, or to achieve a special effect.

With the wonderful diversity of containers available, there is scope for enormous creativity in choosing and planting them so that they may add their own special touch to the garden, large or small. There is no doubt that containers will bring a sense of completion to any garden, and while they may seem expensive, keep in mind that they are going to last a life-time and become an integral part of your garden.

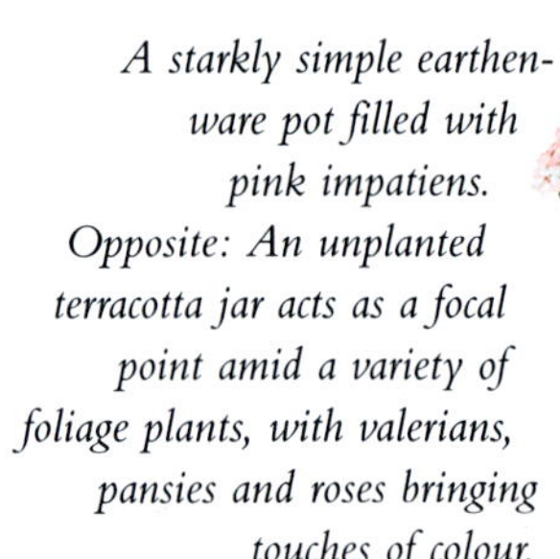

A starkly simple earthenware pot filled with pink impatiens. Opposite: An unplanted terracotta jar acts as a focal point amid a variety of foliage plants, with valerians, pansies and roses bringing touches of colour.

CHAPTER 1

Planning for Containers

Containers call for a special type of gardening. Although you are restricted in size and scope, you can derive immense pleasure from this small-scale garden all year round. To make the most of it, a container garden must be as meticulously planned as any normal garden – not only in terms of the positioning of plants and containers, but also with regard to planting schemes for individual containers. The placing of containers, or groups of containers, should always have a purpose – to brighten up a patio or a space in the garden, or perhaps for the pleasure of bringing outstanding plants together, the impact of which might be lost in the garden. Whatever the purpose, both plants and containers should be chosen for their suitability – for sunny, shady, or windy conditions – and for the way in which they fit into the overall design of the garden or patio. When combining containers and plants several important factors should be borne in mind, namely style, structure, proportion and shape, height and scale, as well as colour of both pots and plants. Keep the basic lines of design simple and use accessories for balance or to create a theme.

Crimson "Little Red Hedge" rose and impatiens, blue lobelias and pink begonias make a colourful picture.

Style

First, decide whether you want to create a formal or an informal look. Formal means elegant, restrained, a symmetry of placing, a design characterized by straight lines. Informal implies a happy abundance of plants cascading, with no apparent symmetry of planting or placing.

The choice of plants and containers should reflect the style and mood of their setting. A Victorian country garden will be enhanced by hanging baskets and windowboxes filled with

pelargoniums, ivies and chlorophytum (hen and chicken). Bamboos in tall pots will create an oriental look, while palms and ferns will bring about a tropical atmosphere. Complement a Mediterranean setting with lavenders, roses, rosemary and verbena in terracotta pots. A high-tech setting calls for the stark, bold shapes of dracaenas and yuccas in geometrically shaped containers which will look decidedly out of place in a rambling country garden. The style that you choose will be influenced by and should harmonize with the style of the house. Also bear in mind the style of furniture used on patios and balconies and in sitting-out areas, and choose containers and plants that will harmonize with this.

An old chimney pot planted with ivy and two pedestals with ornamental pots backed by attractive wrought iron break the monotony of a long wall.

Structure

Container plants can be used to good effect to provide structure on the patio or in the garden. When choosing the plants, decide whether they will be background plants, accent plants, or plants for unity or contrast, colour and variety. Background plants are mainly trees, large shrubs and climbers. The abundant use of climbers may soften harsh surfaces and hard edges and provide a permanent backdrop for further planting. In addition to hiding the boundaries of a patio or sitting-out area, climbing foliage will also provide a lush, luxuriant link with the rest of the garden, creating an illusion of space.

Below: Pinks of several shades create a harmonious frame for a door set into a garden wall.

To avoid a monotonous all-green background, select variegated species and plants with different leaf shapes and textures.

Great care must be taken when choosing the permanent residents for containers. Bear in mind that plants used for background and structure must look good all year round. Evergreens are a safe choice, although deciduous trees and shrubs will have a mist of green in spring, heavy green in summer and, in autumn, provide a magnificent display of rich colours. To add interest to the structure, a mixture of trees, shrubs and climbers can be underplanted with a selection of flowering annuals and bulbs.

Large slabs of paving can be monotonous. Use strategically placed containers filled with interesting foliage plants and annuals to break this monotony. Small pots filled with the same groundcover tumbling down the side will soften a wide flight of steps, while still leaving enough room for traffic.

Accent plants should be chosen for their distinctive, unusual or striking leaf form, shape or colouring that will make them the focus of attention. They can be used singly to display attractive specimen plants, in pairs to frame a view or flight of steps, or in small groups to link house and garden. A wide variety of palms, tree ferns, yuccas, phormiums and cordylines – or topiary in different shapes – can be used as accent plants to add structure to an otherwise featureless part of the garden or patio.

An accent plant placed in a group should be highlighted in some way – either by planting it in a decorative container or by raising it to a higher level than the rest of the grouping.

Proportion and Shape

Plants and containers should complement each other in both shape and size. Floral artists usually keep to a set formula, namely that an arrangement should be one and a half times or twice as high as the container. This is a good proportion for container plants as well: the size of the container should be about a third of the overall height of the combination.

Plants should look comfortable in their containers, not out of place. A huge dieffenbachia will look silly in a small plastic pot, as will a tiny maidenhair fern in a large wooden half-barrel.

Proportion is also important in respect of the area where containers and plants are to be placed. Tall-growing plants in large containers will be more effective around the poolside, while smaller containers with low-growing or trailing plants should be used to line a flight of steps with container-grown plants.

A group of small containers will be difficult to arrange, and will probably look insignificant, whereas one or two substantial containers, or a combination of large and small pots will have more impact.

The basic plant shapes are vertical, oval, dome or round, fan-shaped, horizontal or spreading, and asymmetrical. Containers also come in a large variety of shapes (*see* p. 21) and the shape of the plant and that of the container should always harmonize with and complement each other. A tall, slender-growing conifer will look out of place in a wide Corinthian wall pot, whereas a good-sized pelargonium with trailing ivy around the edges will complement the pot and add life to a dull wall. Buxus looks lovely in an elegant stone urn, less so in a shallow concrete dish. If a tall, narrow container is planted with a slender, upright-growing plant, this will create a tall, vertical line which should be broken by surrounding it with cascading plants. The angular lines of a plant may also be softened by curves in its container, and vice versa.

A long flight of steps is enhanced by ivy and a series of containers planted with impatiens.

Proportion and plant shapes within the same container or a group of containers are equally important – try to achieve a good mix of tall and low-growing, upright and bushy plants. Contrast columnar conifers with the rounded shape of syzygium or other shrubs. Tall and spiky plants can be underplanted with spreading, lower-growing bushes or trailers. Use plants with strong shapes for architectural interest – either on their own or for contrast. Try to achieve a balance between bold, sword-leafed plants such as yuccas, palms, and phormiums, and fine-leafed ferns, bamboos, and ornamental

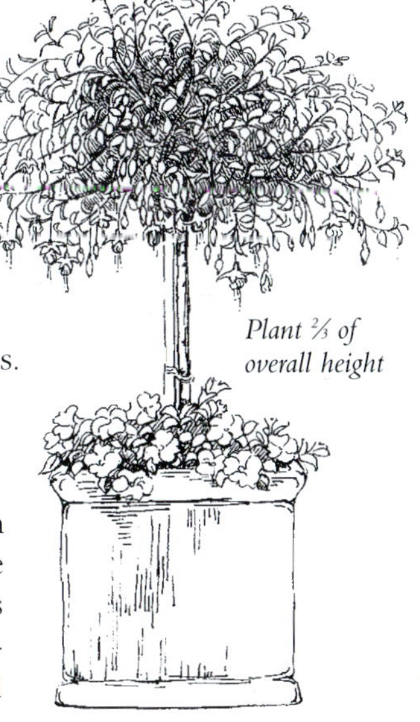

Grey-leafed kalanchoe cascades over a classic urn on a pedestal surrounded by scented pelargoniums.

Below: Sun-loving nierembergia set in a stone pot.

grasses. Combine them with round-leafed plants and ivies, both plain and variegated. Foliage is a very important aspect of planting and while you should certainly look at the quality of flowers, the form and texture of leaves are equally important. Plenty of contrast in shape, size, colour and texture has a lively effect. Plants with subtly or starkly varying leaf shapes grown in the same container can also complement one another.

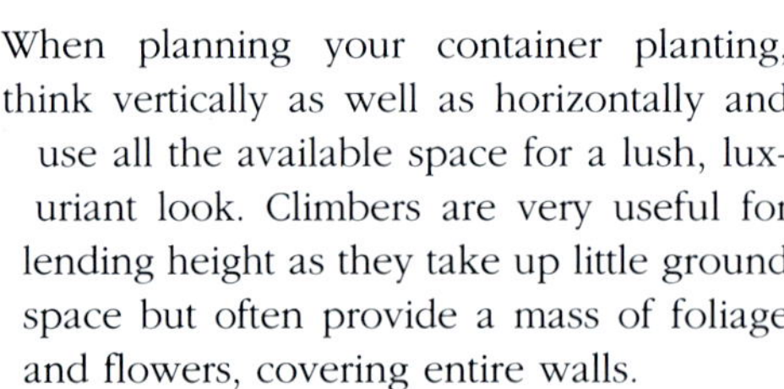

Height and Scale

When planning your container planting, think vertically as well as horizontally and use all the available space for a lush, luxuriant look. Climbers are very useful for lending height as they take up little ground space but often provide a mass of foliage and flowers, covering entire walls.

Different heights add interest to groupings – groups of only tall and narrow or all low and flat containers and plants will be boring. Using raised containers not only adds depth to a planting scheme, but enables you to derive the maximum benefit from a small space. By adding height you extend your garden vertically, showing off the plants to best advantage. Various heights also allow you to show off accent plants, and to include colour at different levels – an important factor in the overall look of a planting scheme.

In the garden, planted containers can be used to create attractive changes of level. A tall, elegant urn, or a container filled with trailing ivy, placed on a pedestal, will lend height to a long border if placed towards the centre. You can also use pedestals or tall containers to raise small, scented plants off the ground for better appreciation of their fragrance.

Scale is important when plants and containers are used to lend height and create different levels. For example, while trees must be of a good size, they should not completely overshadow other plants. A good-sized tree with lower-growing plants under it, could create a pretty picture, even if the lower-growing plants are overshadowed. However, the accompanying plants should be of the right size – smaller versions of the same tree would look out of proportion, whereas smaller shade lovers such as primulas, low-growing impatiens and selaginella in low containers will look natural.

If containers are used to accentuate the change of level at the top of a flight of steps, they will only be effective if they are of good size – three or four times the height of the step, or a quarter of the width. A greater perception of height will be attained if tall plants are used, but tall plants in tall containers can take on a sparse, spindly look, and should be interspersed with low containers planted with more substantial foliage plants.

Colour

Flowers in pots can be used to add extra colour to a planting scheme or to brighten up a dull corner of the garden or patio. There is a multitude of colours to choose from when planning your container planting.

Although it is often said that colours do not clash in nature, and certainly a riot of bright colours can be a delight, it is nevertheless worth taking a look at the advantages of planned colour. Large groups of different colours in a bed

THE COLOUR WHEEL

Of great help is the colour wheel. Make your own version by placing the three primary colours, red, blue and yellow, at three points equidistant on a circle with 12 segments. Between these, place the secondary colours resulting from mixing two primary colours – violet (between blue and red), orange (between red and yellow) and green (between blue and yellow), with the intermediate shades in between. From this you will see which colours blend, and which contrast with one another. All, or any two, primary colours will be a striking combination, as will a combination of the secondary colours, green, violet and orange. Complementary colours are those opposite each other on the wheel, such as green and red, violet and yellow, blue and orange. Then there are the so-called non-colours – white and grey – and neutral colours – beige and brown. White and grey can provide contrast or knit together other colours, while beige is a useful background colour. Keep this in mind when deciding which colours to bring together in the containers.

or border can be brought together by pale yellow, blue or grey, to make a harmonious whole, but for containers, plants must be carefully selected for a pleasing appearance and to ensure that there is no unhappy clashing of colours.

Although a colour scheme may look good on paper, it may go awry, owing to the many shades, tints and tones present in one colour. Orange, for instance, could be reddish, yellowish or brownish; yellow may be lemon or gold; red could be scarlet or a deep crimson-burgundy. For this reason it is best to keep the colour scheme simple – too many colours splashed around may detract from the overall beauty of the container garden. A monochromatic scheme means the bringing together of flowers of one colour. A patio, or a gazebo, hung about with baskets of pink flowers, with pink flowers growing in and cascading from other containers can look wonderful provided that the shades are chosen carefully – for example, salmon pink and blue pink may not look good together. The prevalent

Unplanted containers and pipes of startling blue, and an uncluttered water-feature create a modern look in a shaded garden.

colours in background and accent plants can be echoed in smaller plants chosen as their companions. The principles of colour grouping apply to containers as much as in the garden. Cool colours, such as blue, mauve or grey, in the distance, will extend the space and create the impression of depth, making a patio, for instance, seem larger, whereas warm colours – bright oranges and reds – will have the opposite effect.

Bear in mind that colour does not only come from flowers – foliage plants with golden, blue, silver-grey or variegated leaves play an important role and should be used to complement or contrast with flowering plants. Plants with silver-grey leaves are a beautiful foil for pink, blue and purple flowering plants, and variegated plants can bring their own splashes of colour or, in a dark corner, create the illusion of dappled sunlight.

Tall, slender lavender stands proud of a tumbling of felicia and verbenas in shades of soft lilac.

Positioning

Positioning of containers needs a great deal of thought, and it is well worthwhile looking at books, or other people's gardens, to see what would appeal to you and suit your needs.

You should look not only at the overall design and appearance of the garden and house, but also bear in mind several practical considerations. The background against which containers will be placed must be considered: an old-fashioned, decorative urn may be beautiful in its own right, and ideal as a focal point in the garden, but will look out of place against a stark, geometrically shaped wall. A wooden tub planted with hydrangeas and overflowing with trailing ivies will be attractive on the verandah of a country-style house, but look odd against a modern setting of glass and aluminium.

The intensity and movement of the sun, as well as prevalent winds and other climatic conditions such as frost, are important considerations, as they affect the health of your plants. Containers should be placed in such a way that the plants will always obtain the maximum benefit from their micro-climate.

Container-grown plants should be placed where they can be admired and enjoyed without cluttering up a sitting-out area or patio. When containers are placed on patios, or are used to frame steps, or as a focal point at the meeting of paths, position them in such a way that the plants will not be damaged by passing traffic.

Grouping

When grouped together, the most diverse assortment of pots and plants can achieve an unexpected unity. It is good to experiment with grouping and planting to achieve this, as you may find that once the containers are in place, they take on a different appearance when they are planted. It is a good idea to arrange the containers according to plan and place new plants in their bags into the containers to see how they look, before planting them. Colours may not be right, textures may not go well together, shapes may not work. This temporary placement will help greatly in finalizing the arrangement.

Generally, it is better to group containers of the same material, although such a grouping may be monotonous if the containers are all of the same shape and size. And if you have a beautiful container of outstanding shape, or with intricate decoration, it would be a pity to detract from its beauty by surrounding it with containers of a lower standard. Rather place it on its own where it can be seen at its best.

Containers of plants which bloom at the same time can be brought together in season. Camellias come into bloom with primulas, and large pots planted with a mass of *Primula malacoides* can be grouped with camellias planted in their own pots.

On the patio, when climbers such as clematis and wisteria are in bloom, the addition of hanging baskets overflowing with petunias, lobelia and alyssum will create a festive air. In summer, when large tubs of hydrangeas are in full bloom in the semi-shade, impatiens, begonias and ferns placed at different levels will add a cool, moist look. These containers can be moved elsewhere when the hydrangeas die down.

Accessories

Once you have achieved a satisfactory grouping, you may find that it needs a little something to round off the arrangement. Sculptural stones and pebbles can be used to great effect, and a statue or pedestal will lend height. Concrete birds and animals also go well with groups of container plants. Two or three tree stumps of different height, or an interestingly shaped piece of wood may complete the picture.

Water in a container placed among the plants will add to the vitality of containerized plants and bring welcome moisture to the atmosphere. Moving water, in particular, creates a tranquil atmosphere, and electric pumps used for this purpose are easy to install.

Planting Schemes

Containers can be moved around to create different effects during different seasons, or individual plants in containers replaced after blooming, or when they become straggly and untidy.

When planning your planting, you should have both short and long-term schemes for seasonal impact and colour all year round against the backdrop of a permanent structure. Short-term schemes will revolve mainly around bulbs and annuals, whereas trees, shrubs and climbers are more permanent and will constitute long-term schemes. You can have both short and long-term plants in the same container, for example a tree or standard underplanted with annuals which are changed seasonally.

Thorough planning of your container planting and placement will ensure that all the elements you use form an attractive and cohesive whole in harmony with the setting.

Left: A grouping of tree stumps and ethnic pots, surrounded by the architectural shapes of agave and phormium, make a suitable accompaniment for sleeper steps.

Below: Examples of the wide variety of accessories available.

Simple shapes surrounded by simple flowers: daisies, forget-me-nots and geraniums. Opposite: Containers of pastel shades host plumbago, streptocarpus, petunias and impatiens, backed by a Natalian bougainvillea.

CHAPTER 2

Choosing a Container

Containers are available in a vast range of shapes, sizes and colours, and may range from a few centimetres high planted with a small cactus, to giant urns, Aladdin jars and troughs, gracing the patio or other parts of the garden. Windowboxes and hanging baskets are particularly attractive and are often the only gardening space available to flat-dwellers, and therefore the main tool for balcony gardens. In a highly decorative container, plants will play a subordinate role; on the other hand, very plain plastic and concrete pots will have to be imaginatively planted to make sure that they don't look dull and uninteresting. Investing in interesting and decorative containers, whether purpose-made or improvised, will certainly be worth your while, as they can set the scene and improve the overall look of your patio and garden.

A hole cut in the side of a suspended gourd allows for the planting of a cascading lobelia.

Materials

When selecting a container, bear in mind how and where it will be used – should it be lightweight, portable, large, small, decorative or simple? Many materials are used for containers, each with its advantages and disadvantages. The material chosen should be attractive and blend well with the design of the house and patio. For example, terracotta will look attractive with the warm colours of brick and wood, not so with the greys of concrete slabs.

Also consider the porosity of the material you choose, as this, in turn, affects watering and drainage. Good drainage is essential in all containers. Unglazed clay, terracotta and untreated wood are porous materials that water and air will penetrate. Plastic, metal, glazed terracottas and fibreglass are non-porous and will have no air and water penetration. In porous materials the soil dries out quickly, so plants will need more frequent watering. Non-porous materials hold water better, but need special care with drainage to prevent plants from becoming waterlogged.

Fibre cement is fairly light, making it relatively easy to move, but care should be taken not to damage the containers when they are moved. Fibre-cement containers and garden accessories are available in a large variety of shapes and sizes, and are easy to paint or decorate. Because of its alkalinity, acid-loving plants do not take kindly to being planted in fibre cement. If you want to plant an acid-lover in a fibre-cement pot, line the container with plastic, making sure that you allow for good drainage.

Terracotta is of the earth, and so blends well with the garden and home, and many ceramic artists are turning to this form of containers. These containers are either glazed or unglazed and come in various sizes and shapes, often with matching drip trays. They are extremely attractive and ideal for creating a Mediterranean or tropical look. Terracotta is porous, and plants in unglazed containers will need more frequent watering than, for example, in plastic pots. Terracotta is also a naturally brittle material which may easily crack and break, and needs to be handled with great care. Although terracotta keeps the soil cool, the roots of plants may suffer from frost during winter. Except for very plain containers, terracotta is expensive. Look for the many convincing, far cheaper imitations available, or paint fibre cement or plastic pots terracotta colour.

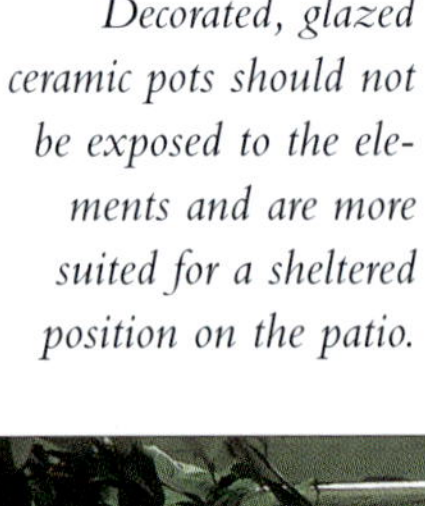

Decorated, glazed ceramic pots should not be exposed to the elements and are more suited for a sheltered position on the patio.

Ceramic containers are very attractive, and many of them are works of art in their own right. Finding suitable plants for them may be a little difficult, especially if they are highly coloured, and often it is better to keep to one plant, especially green foliage, to plant in them. Ceramic is susceptible to frost, and precious containers should not be exposed to the elements.

Wood is a natural material, with a look of nature, and is used for tubs, barrels, windowboxes, planters and hanging baskets. Most wooden containers look particularly attractive in country surroundings, while squared-off wooden tubs are attractive in formal settings. Wood helps to keep the roots of growing plants warm, but requires more maintenance than most other containers. Left untreated and exposed to the elements, it will deteriorate quickly, and eventually rot. It can be varnished, painted or treated with wood preservatives that are not toxic to plants, and should be singed with a blowlamp to make it less susceptible to damp. A lining of plastic will also help to preserve wood. Do not use creosote as the fumes may harm plants. Always stand wooden containers off the ground – on special container feet available from nurseries or garden shops, or bricks, so that air can pass through underneath to stop the wood from rotting. Wooden containers are easy to make yourself – use hardwood that will last longer.

Plastic is now one of the most popular materials for containers as it is cheap, versatile, light to handle and bends rather than breaks. Plastic containers are moulded into all kinds of shapes, including tower pots which slot into one another with plants growing out of the sides – similar to a strawberry planter. It is not porous and holds water longer, but take care, for plants in plastic containers may become waterlogged. Pelargoniums should not be planted in plastic containers

Containers finely moulded in concrete on the left, draped pots on the right, and below, an ornamental barrow planted with pink petunias and silene.

for this reason. The main disadvantage is that plastic may become brittle from exposure to sun and water, and may crack after a while – but then they are not very expensive to replace.

Fibreglass is much more expensive than plastic, but far stronger and more durable. It is often moulded to look like lead, stone or other materials – in the classic shapes of decorative urns and troughs. The biggest disadvantage is the initial cost, but fibreglass containers will last a lifetime.

Metal. Lovely old containers of lead are much sought after and almost impossible to obtain, but containers of iron, copper and brass are more readily available. Old kitchen coppers eventually develop an attractive green patina. On the whole, these are used more as outer containers, the plants being placed, in their pots, inside the container. Old buckets and cooking pots can have holes drilled in them to allow for drainage. Lately, buckets and cans of galvanized iron, painted bright colours, have come on the market, which will happily brighten up their part of the garden or patio. Unpainted galvanized containers should be specially treated before painting them.

Concrete containers come in many diverse shapes, from old and antique containers, such as ornate urns, pots and troughs to the more mod-

ern cones, bowls and squares. Many of these containers are available with intricate and finely detailed moulds of leaf and other shapes. Concrete is rather heavy, and it is advisable to place large containers in position before filling and planting them. They will have to stay put once they are in position. Acid-loving plants will require a plastic lining to keep them happy in concrete containers.

Tufa containers are made of a porous stone-mix and have a lovely old-world look. A substitute can be made by mixing equal quantities of cement, coarse, clean sand and either shredded coir or peatmoss. Use this mixture to cover plastic or other containers, or for moulding new ones.

Right: A selection of Everite fibre-cement pots painted in various colours, including terracotta.

Below: The selection of foliage used in the planting of old china jugs and dishes does not detract from the charm of these unusual containers.

Other Ideas

Anything that can hold soil in which a plant will grow can be a container, provided that it will also complement the plant with its shape, size, colour and texture. You should therefore always be on the look-out for suitable containers. Hollowed out logs, tree stumps, earthenware pipes, old chimney pots, African grinding stones, and hollowed rocks are among the many objects which may be introduced as containers for planting. Old sinks, large tins or oil cans painted in bright colours, old wooden wheelbarrows and water tanks of various sizes could make interestingly different containers.

Try a bird bath planted with colourful annuals or other container plants with a shallow root system, or an old wicker doll's pram filled with plastic pots of trailing ivy and gaily flowering impatiens. Browsing through junk shops and scrap-metal yards can yield a host of ideas for containers ... the possibilities are endless.

Basic Requirements

When choosing a container, the size and shape of the container must be balanced by the size and shape of the plants.

It must have adequate drainage, not be too heavy for the purpose for which you want to use it, and complement the style and character of the house or patio.

Size

Always try to choose containers as large as possible as they make a bigger impact and require less frequent watering. Essentially, a container must be big enough to hold enough soil and compost to meet the needs of the plants it will house. If the container is too big, the plants will look lost in it. If it is too small, the nutrients are quickly used up and plants may become root-bound which impedes healthy growth.

Depth may vary greatly to suit various plants, and when choosing plants for certain containers, proportion and scale should always be taken into account. A good ratio is regarded as the plant being one and a half times or twice the height of the container (*see* p. 11).

A container should also be tall enough to comfortably accommodate the roots of the proposed plant. Some plants, such as conifers, have long tap roots, so should have deeper containers than those with superficial roots, such as azaleas and camellias whose roots should be given space to spread out and which will need wider containers. Allowance must, of course, be made for the potential future growth of the plant. But, conversely, placing a tiny plant into a large contain-

SHAPE	SUGGESTED PLANTING
Classic urn	Trailing ivy with a dwarf conifer in the centre or a small topiary tree, well clipped and unaccompanied or a mixture of *Helichrysum petiolare* and ivy-leafed pelargoniums
Sculptural	Echeveria or trailing ivy or a mass of petunias or white liliums with blue pansies
Wineglass shape	*Begonia semperflorens* and blue and white lobelia or *Chlorophytum comosum* or *Felicia amelloides* and brachycome daisy
Cylindrical	Conifer "Sky Rocket" edged with white or mauve alyssum or blue lobelias or for wider pot *Argyranthemum frutescens* with ivy-leafed pelargonium or "Pink Sunsation" rose with scaevola
Grecian pot or wall-mounted half-tub	Variegated ivy such as "Glacier" with white petunias or red and purple verbena or white cascading petunias or lavender
Corinthian pot or wall-mounted half-tub	Variegated vinca with yellow violas or ivy-leafed pelargonium or "Surfinia" petunias
Wooden container, square	Conifer "Donard Gold" with yellow pansies or vinca or lysimachia (creeping Jenny) or white standard azalea with blue lobelias
Wooden container, round	Hydrangeas or standard "Fairy" rose with white violas or standard fuchsia "Billy Green" with cascading fuchsias "Pink Galore" or several white daisy bushes with pink cascading petunias around the edge
Flute pot	*Nandina domestica* "Pigmaea" with ivy or clipped *Murraya exotica* standard edged with impatiens
Quarter segment pot	*Euonymus fortunei* "Emerald Gaiety" with green trailing vinca or ivy-leafed pelargonium with variegated ivy "Glacier"
Regency pot	Red zonal pelargoniums Red tulips with white *Primula malacoides*

Fittonia, tillandsia, tradescantia, and callisia make an attractive hairdo for an elegant lady.

er could result in the soil turning sour, and also a lack of proportion. Plants like to be comfortable in their containers, so it is better to buy a plant which fits, or almost fits, its container, then keeping its roots contained by regular clipping back. One thing to avoid when choosing a pot for a plant which is going to grow fairly large, and which will eventually have to be repotted, is a pot with an opening smaller than its general width, such as an Aladdin jar. When the time comes to remove the plant, it will be almost impossible to get the root ball through the narrow neck, as the roots would have taken on the shape of the container surrounding them.

Shape

Certain shapes of containers lend themselves to certain types of plants which may be cascading, upright, round, slender, or low-growing. Careful choice of the container will ensure a well-balanced look. Traditional shapes for containers include Drostdy pots and tubs – an elegant choice for tall specimens such as conifers. Contemporary geometric designs are starker, and will complement the bold, strong leaf forms of yuccas and cordylines. There are special, flat, cone-shaped pots for cacti and other succulents, allowing for a fairly shallow root system, but with lots of surface space. Strawberry planters, with various openings in the side, are not exclusively for strawberries: plant them with herbs or annuals, or a mixture of trailing ivies, herbs and annuals. A clay wall pot resembling a swallow's nest will need nothing more than a small foliage plant for a lovely and unusual display.

A chimney pot and containers of various shapes, painted in terracotta, planted with pink impatiens and begonias, and blue campanula.

Round ethnic pots, especially those which have been decorated, are best used as a decoration only. Tall, slender ethnic pots can be planted with trailing succulents such as kalanchoes, or an upright-growing aloe. Oriental pots are usually highly decorated and are better planted with a plant with simple lines. The table on page 21 contains some suggestions for further container and plant combinations.

Drainage

Good drainage is essential for good growth, so drainage holes in containers are vital. When you buy a container, examine its bottom to see if there are sufficient drainage holes for water to flow out freely, and that they are not blocked. The garden shop will probably obligingly drill more, if necessary, or you can enlarge the existing ones. The holes should be at or near the base, and at least 1 cm in diameter.

Bigger pots (deeper than 30 cm) should have drainage holes of at least 2 cm in diameter, about 15 cm apart. The bigger the pot, the more drainage holes are required. Drilling of these holes requires proper tools to avoid damage to the containers, and should not be attempted without the right equipment.

Raising containers off a flat surface will certainly aid drainage and aeration. Some pots and windowboxes have built-in feet, and special container feet are available from most nurseries for those which don't. You can also use small blocks of wood, always making sure that the container is level and stands firmly.

Weight

This is an important consideration – if containers are to be moved around frequently, they should not be too heavy. For balconies, it is better to look at lightweight containers such as plastic. If wind is prevalent, lighter containers may be blown over and need to be anchored.

Complementing the setting

Containers must not only complement their planting, but also the materials, and style and character, of their setting. If a pot is to be placed on a pedestal, the style of the pedestal should match that of the pot. Modern, geometric shapes will complement a modern and high-tech house, while wooden barrels and wicker baskets will suit a country cottage, and moss-covered urns and stone tubs an older, classical home.

In the garden terracotta, with its natural look, will blend beautifully, but stone which has been aged, and fibre cement will also do well. Also make sure that the containers match the floor surface of the patio or sitting-out area – terracotta may clash with some shades of red brick tiles, but will look attractive on tiles or paving of a lighter colour. Wooden barrels are lovely on a wooden deck and brick paving, less so on cement paving.

Practical Considerations

Choose sturdy, all-weather containers for the garden where they will be exposed to the elements. In frosty areas, containers should not be prone to icy conditions.

Containers, new as well as used, must be cleaned thoroughly before use. New porous, non-glazed containers may need a good soak in clean water to ensure that harmful salts which may be present are dissolved and removed and that the container is hydrated – dried-out pots will absorb too much moisture from the soil.

Make sure that containers stand firmly and crock them properly to encourage good aeration and drainage and to prevent fine soil from being washed out of the container. Also bear in mind how the material of the containers you choose affects maintenance. Plants in a plastic container need less water than those in porous terracotta which absorbs water.

Containers must be made stable so that children cannot pull them over. Also make sure that tall plants in tall containers will not be blown over by the wind, by placing it in a sheltered position, or anchoring it with a sturdy stake.

Windowboxes

At one time windowboxes were just that – plant boxes attached to windowsills – but now this term includes long troughs which may be placed on the patio, or suspended from walls away from the windows. Those which are suspended should be of a material that is not too heavy, such as wood or asbestos, and the supports used must be sturdy and secure. The best way to prevent surplus water from spoiling the walls or floor surface, is to place each suspended pot in its own tray. Another way of dealing with this is to place a box within a box, for example, a plastic container may be placed, on feet, within a wooden outer container.

Long, narrow containers resembling windowboxes and placed on the patio may be bought ready-made, or can be built out of bricks, in which case weep-holes must be allowed for. An interesting alternative for a windowbox effect is a row of galvanized buckets filled with brightly flowering plants, suspended from a sturdy structure below a windowsill. Drainage holes should be drilled before filling the buckets with soil.

Windowboxes and hanging baskets turn a dull wall into an attractive feature.

Suspended Containers

Suspended containers of different shapes, sizes and colours can be very attractive and offer you the opportunity to display plants and colours at different levels. Frequent watering will be required, so don't place them over a sitting area or where there will be a lot of traffic.

Baskets are usually made of wire, but suspended containers also include plastic bowls, containers of wooden slats and woven baskets or wicker baskets. An important factor is the weight of suspended containers, and the hooks and wire from which they are suspended, and the material used must be sturdy and strong. Place a fisherman's swivel between the basket and the wire from which it is suspended to prevent twisting of the wire and to allow the basket to hang freely.

A fisherman's swivel prevents too much twisting between a hanging basket and the wire from which it is suspended.

Plastic bowls may simply be filled with soil and planted, but wire baskets need a little extra attention. They should be lined with plastic sheeting, special ready-made liners, shade cloth or moss.

An easy method to prepare a basket is to line it with coir, about 5 cm thick, slightly tamped down. Cut a piece of plastic to cover the bottom of the container, coming up the sides a little; place this over the coir. Fill with a good soil mixture, incorporating a moisture retainer, such as *Osmocote* or *Terrasorb*, and fill with plants. Slits can be made in the sides into which seedlings can be inserted.

Right: A symphony of pink petunias, roses and silene flourishing in the light shade of a pergola.

Hanging baskets are often seen from below, so cascading plants are ideal – fuchsias with a trailing growth make splendid subjects, as do ivies, begonias, pelargoniums and many annuals.

You can also mount a trellis to a wall, with baskets, pots and buckets of plants suspended at different heights. Any structure used to suspend containers must be strong enough to take the weight.

Painting Containers

Most containers can be painted and this has the advantage that you can colour match them to your home and patio furniture. They can also be painted if you prefer a colour different from the original coating, or if you want to change a colour scheme. The imaginative use of colour and paint techniques can turn an ordinary container into an exclusive feature.

If there is moulding on a pot, this can be painted a different colour, or alternatively, an attractive effect can be brought about by rubbing the high points of the moulding free of paint, then painting them lightly with gold or silver.

Any good quality PVA paint is suitable for container painting. Everite has developed a high quality acrylic PVA paint, especially for containers, and this is available to the general public in economical 500 ml tins under the *Everite Pot Paint* brandname. These paints are ideally suited for special paint techniques such as rag painting, sponging, dribbling, marbling and stencilling. Mat paints are more suitable, unless you want to achieve a lacquered effect.

Before painting any container, make sure that it is spotlessly clean and that all traces of grease, dust and other particles have been removed. Paint the pot one colour, or use one of the following paint techniques to achieve a different effect.

Rag painting

Rag painting will bring about a soft, antique look. Apply a good coat of paint in a slightly darker or lighter colour than the colour you chose for rag painting and allow to dry completely. Use mutton cloth rolled up into a sausage shape, roll this into the second colour of paint (pouring the paint into a flat dish will facilitate the process), and roll the sausage onto a thick layer of paper towels to get rid of excess paint. Now roll the sausage across the surface of the container in short movements, constantly changing direction to avoid repeat patterns. Continue until the entire surface of the container has been covered.

Sponging

Sponging gives a more textured finish and is useful for achieving a granite look. Apply a base coat and allow to dry, as for rag painting. Use a natural sea sponge, wet thoroughly and squeeze out excess water. Dip the sponge into the paint chosen, and dab off excess paint on a thick layer of paper towels. Gently dab the sponge onto the surface of the container, taking care not to drag your hand. Change direction all the time to avoid a repeat pattern, and repeat this process until the entire surface of the container has been covered.

Colours

The choice of colour will depend on personal taste, but here are some pointers: Windowboxes with brick patterns to resemble a brick raised bed, should be painted in a brick colour. Similarly, imitation wooden half-barrels should be painted in wood colour for authenticity. Painting concrete and fibre-cement containers in terracotta colour can achieve that luxuriant terracotta look at a fraction of the price, although these containers may not last as long as the real thing.

Beige is a good neutral colour if you don't want a container to detract from the beauty of the plants. Green could show off plants beautifully, but is a difficult colour to use as it could clash terribly with the green of the plants. It is safer to use a dark green for pots. Try a small patch on the pot and if the result is too startling, buy a small tin of black paint and add this, a little at a time, to the green, until a soothing deep green with no hint of yellow is achieved.

Making Your Own

You can make your own containers if you are of that turn of mind. Wood can be cut to specifications and joined, and moulds made for concrete containers. Tufa containers have become popular and are easy to make yourself (*see* p. 20).

MAKING YOUR OWN CONCRETE TROUGH

It is quite easy to make your own concrete trough. Use two wooden boxes, one larger than the other. Paint the bigger box with cooking oil on the inside and pour about 5 – 7,5 cm of concrete into its base. Press metal tubes into the concrete for drainage holes. Paint the smaller box with cooking oil on the outside and place it exactly in the middle of the bigger one on top of the concrete just before it has set – make sure that the space between the boxes is 5 – 7 cm wide – and pour concrete into the space between the boxes. Strip off the wood as soon as the concrete has set.

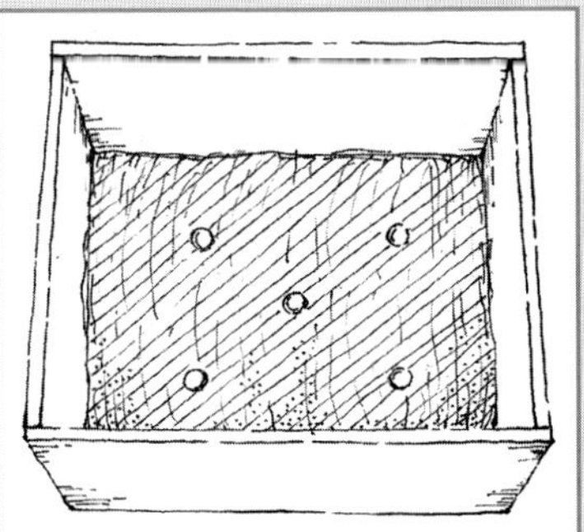

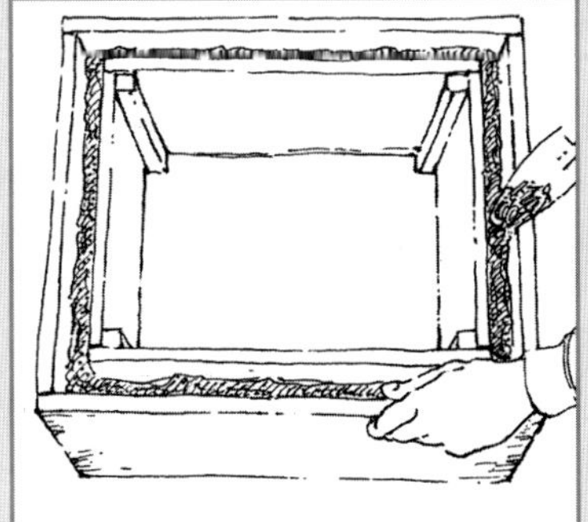

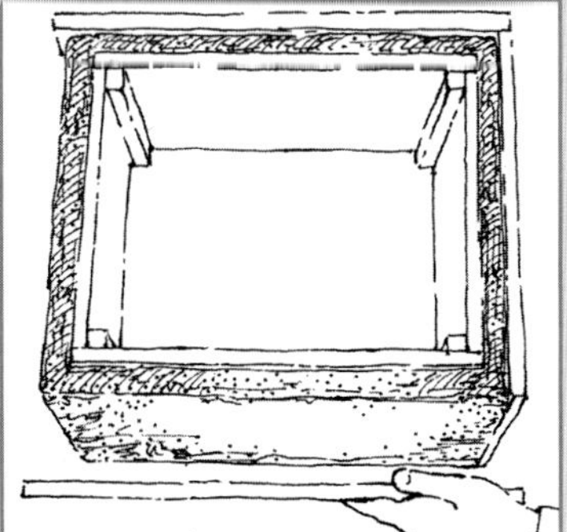

A colourful array of begonias lends a festive air to the pool area. Opposite: White petunias and silene overflow a shallow container on a stone pedestal surrounded by a variety of white flowers in the ground.

CHAPTER 3

Containers in the Garden

Containers have a distinctive role to play in any garden – large or small. One of the biggest advantages of containers is their versatility and their extensive use will increase your design options. With container plants, you are able to control their environment and introduce plants normally not suitable for your soil or climate, use your background to advantage, create areas of interest with decorative containers, grouping, colour and focal points, and turn problem areas into delightful as well as practical places to relax and enjoy your garden.

Ixora and bromeliads create an exotic effect. These are essentially for a frost-free garden.

Changing the Aspect

Provided the containers are not too heavy, you can change the overall aspect of your garden or a section of the garden which has become boring simply by moving them around, or by replanting a few containers to provide instant seasonal colour. If you wish to move very heavy containers, it is usually possible to hire or borrow a special trolley or barrow from your nursery or garden centre, or there are special container movers on the market (*see* p. 124).

Controlling the Environment

Containers enable you to grow plants otherwise not suited to the type of soil in your garden. Because you can control the environment of container-grown plants to a large degree, you can give each plant the soil it prefers and in which it will thrive.

Acid-loving plants such as azaleas and camellias can be given their own supply of acid soil when planted in a large container or barrel, and placed in a protected semi-shaded position.

Cacti and succulents need full sun and extremely good drainage, and they will often not fit into a mixed border. But if you fill a container with a collection of attractive succulents, their specific needs can be met and yet they can still be part of the garden.

Plants such as astilbes and Louisiana irises need plenty of water during their growing season and, unlike many other plants, don't mind boggy conditions which can be brought about by planting them in their own containers.

Positioning

An important factor to consider when using containers in the garden is that they are open to the elements. Those containing plants that are vulnerable to wind or rain should therefore be placed in the most sheltered position, while tougher plants should be chosen for containers in exposed areas. Both sun-loving plants and shade-loving plants can be given a special place that suits them. Also bear in mind that you can move container-grown plants to protect them against frost or other seasonal climatic conditions.

The clean lines of the urn contrast with the nearby profusion of colourful perennials.

An unattractive wall can be hidden behind a mounted trellis for hanging baskets and pots filled with trailing plants and colourful annuals. An alternative is to suspend pots or baskets of trailing plants from sturdy hooks inserted into the wall itself. Special semi-circular containers are available which are ideal for attaching to a wall and planting with a variety of plants. These, combined with containers at the base of the wall and planted with standards will not only hide the wall, but turn it into an attractive feature.

If there is not enough space for a bed in front of a plain wall, position several containers planted with tall, slender conifers along its length, and you won't even notice the wall.

Don't neglect outbuildings and other structures that may not form part of the garden as such. Just one container-grown plant of good proportion placed against the dividing wall between two garages will detract from its sheer utility.

Creating Different Levels

Containers can be used to create different levels in the garden for added interest. If you have a very long border, an urn placed on a column among the plants towards the centre of the border will give a whole new perspective.

Similarly, a bed of plants of much the same height may appear a little boring – until a column and container, or an elevated container filled with trailing plants, such as ivy, is placed among them. Trees and shrubs in containers can lend height and interest to otherwise featureless areas in the garden.

A peninsular bed, protruding into the lawn, may be made more interesting by the addition of a tall, slender plant in a container placed at the tip of the peninsula.

Decorative Containers

Use containers to make a statement in any area of the garden. Even if they are not planted, many containers are an attractive feature on their own. A gigantic terracotta Aladdin jar, for instance, will need no plants to make a statement at a meeting of paths. Similarly, plants could detract from the artistic shape of an urn placed on a column with a dark green hedge in the background.

Ethnic clay pots, often of a round shape, do not always lend themselves to planting, but make a worthwhile contribution when grouped with other containers. Some ceramic artists specialize in making containers which are in themselves works of art and probably do not need the enhancement of plants.

Grouping of Containers

Grouping several containers in the garden can be a fascinating undertaking. It is not wise to mix too many different materials (for example wood and ceramic), but various shapes – tall and slender, short and round, or flat and square – can be brought together with great effect. And the containers need not all be planted – an empty but decorative container often adds the finishing touch to a visually pleasing grouping.

The addition of a statue or a slender column will often complete the picture. Arrange pebbles, stones and tree stumps around your containers to

Good use has been made of this old plough, which, painted white, makes an attractive and unusual stand for troughs of scarlet pelargoniums.

Create an Olde Worlde Container

If you want your containers and garden ornaments to take on an aged, weathered look, just follow these easy steps: First roughen the surface by scrubbing with a steel or other hard brush, then paint the container or ornament with natural yoghurt or liquid manure. Place it in the shade for a few days, keeping it slightly damp. Soon moss will appear, and your container or ornament will take on an aged look, like an ancient heirloom.

Sutera cascades from two containers on pedestals of dressed stone which define the entrance to an elegant and serene green and white garden.

Below right: A figure supporting a shallow container planted mainly with foliage, links with the white pillar and wrought iron, while in the shade, terracotta containers blend with a brick wall, creating a warm welcome.

achieve a special effect, or use a tree stump instead of a column to elevate a container and create an attractive change of level in the grouping.

Groups of containers can also be used to link the house with the garden. Often a carefully chosen assortment of containers of different heights and shapes grouped together looks far more attractive than any single one would have looked on its own.

Colour

Containers can provide instant seasonal colour merely by changing plantings in some containers as the seasons change. They are a useful tool for 'cheating' in the garden. Merely buy seedlings which are about to flower and place them in containers anywhere in the garden for instant splashes of colour. Some annuals are available in separate bags of a good size, which can simply be placed in a large container with enough soil between them to just cover the bags.

Pay special attention to the colour of containers used in the garden. White tends to stand out, and may be a little startling, whereas terracotta and grey blend more naturally with their surroundings. The colour of structures such as the walls of buildings should also be considered. Weathered containers look attractive against grey or stone walls; terracotta blends well with brick. Trailing plants can be used to camouflage unattractive containers and a coat of paint can give any container an entirely new appearance (*see* p. 24). Many homeowners paint their containers to either blend or contrast with their home, often with delightful and interesting results.

Focal Points

Containers can also be used to create focal points to suit the pattern of natural changes that take place in any garden as a result of growth, seasons, pruning, new plantings, and so forth.

A container can create a focal point at the end of a path, or at the meeting of paths. Containers can be used to define a flight of steps, or a change of level, while wide steps are enhanced by flanking them with container-grown plants. Containers also combine beautifully with statues, benches or ornaments such as bird baths, bringing interest, grace and elegance to special corners of the garden. But the greatest care should be taken not to create an air of clutter which could detract from the individual containers.

Ornate containers placed near or on either side of the front door or entrance to a house will give a warm welcome to guests, and if the container-grown plants are well maintained, also give an indication of what lovely sights may await one in the garden on the other side of the house.

Problem Areas

You may want to make use of the shade of a tree, but find it impossible to plant anything under the tree, as the cultivation of the soil would encourage the roots to come to the surface.

Paving which is kept dry, however, will offer no encouragement to the roots and provide the ideal sitting-out area. A collection of tubs and containers filled with shade-loving plants such as ferns, hostas, impatiens, fuchsias and hydrangeas will add their quota of beauty and interest to your sitting-out area.

Some shrubs have vigorous root systems, and, if planted in a bed together with less robust plants, will soon take over. However, if they are confined to a container and placed in the bed or border, they will not interfere with the other plants and still look good.

A gardener is often frustrated by the knowledge that water and sewerage pipes have been laid under a section of the garden which lends itself to plantings of bright flowers or shrubs. Don't despair – just lay down some flagstones, place on them all manner of containers and fill them with plants to your heart's delight. This also applies to those unsightly but necessary manhole covers. Now, if any work needs to be done, the containers can easily be moved.

When deciduous trees in the garden are bare during winter, and letting the sunlight through, turn them into a special feature by arranging several containers of generous proportions underneath, filled with winter bulbs and annuals: tulips mixed with primulas, or daffodils mixed with alyssum or lobelias, are just two lovely combinations. You can also combine various winter bulbs, such as freesias and ixias, or Dutch irises, daffodils and muscari.

Hanging baskets filled with colourful annuals will liven up the seemingly dead branches of the tree. Petunias, lobelias, alyssum and nemesias will bring bright colour to the winter and early spring scene.

And when summer comes and the trees are in full leaf once more and casting shade, move the hanging baskets elsewhere and plant the containers with a variety of shade lovers such as coleus, impatiens, torenias and violas.

Choosing the Plants

Some plants are seasonal, some are attractive throughout the year. There are plants for shade and plants for sunny parts of the garden. Some are valued for their flowers, some for their foliage, others for their form or texture. There is a vast range of plants to choose from when planning containers for the garden, and it is worthwhile consulting catalogues and books to determine which plants are best for containers in specific parts of the garden. The plant lists in further chapters of this book should also be most useful to help you choose plants for your containers.

Containers around the Pool

A pool bare of surrounding plants looks bare indeed, but poolowners are often loath to plant anything near the pool for fear of vigorous root systems which may damage the pool or paving, unsightly soil which could cause slipping, or leaves and flowers which may pollute the water.

The handsome, shining leaves of crinum lilies are a perfect foil for the beauty of delicately moulded containers, framing the winding path in the shade of large plane trees.

The answer is containers. The biggest advantages are that roots will be contained and, with the use of drip trays, there is no danger of soil or dirty water leaking out onto the surrounding paving and into the pool. Also, containers can be moved away as the plants die down or become untidy.

The choice of plants is great indeed. Palm trees always lend a lovely, tropical look, and don't drop their leaves (*see* p. 99 for examples). Several palms grouped together in containers will bring welcome shade and add a touch of elegance, as will, for example, the Natal wild banana (*Strelitzia nicolai*).

Other suitable tall subjects are cordylines and conifers. Choose plants with decorative foliage to soften the usually stark lines of the pool.

Annuals are a bright addition to pool planting, but their choice should be limited to those with a long blooming season, such as *Begonia semperflorens*, or impatiens. Preferably container-grown plants should not be allowed to cascade over the edge of the container, as spent flowers or dead leaves could cause swimmers to slip.

Certain plants are not recommended. Plants with vicious thorns or spines should be avoided, as should any poisonous plants as it is highly likely that children will be using the pool.

Deciduous trees and shrubs could also be a menace when they drop their leaves. Generally, any plants which tend to be messy should be avoided in the pool area.

Containers used around the pool should be on the generous side to keep to the scale of the pool. A few large containers will be more practical and look more attractive than lots of small ones. The colour of the containers is a personal choice, although it is accepted that white may cause an uncomfortable glare. Containers should be grouped and placed in such a way that they will not interfere with the general traffic.

Initially, the introduction of containers into the garden may seem an expensive undertaking, but they are going to last for a long time, and are sure to become an inherent part of the garden.

Given the versatility of containers, you have the luxury of rearranging and keeping your garden interesting and alive throughout the year, and to reflect both your taste and the dictates of nature year after year.

Opposite: Pink roses, penstemons and oenothera are good companions for the ornate fountain.

Left: A prettily planted gathering of pots at the poolside.

Below: A large furcraea forms a stark contrast with the pink bougainvilleas which blend with the tibouchinas in the background.

"Pink Sunsation" rose is a suitable choice for the wooden half-barrel, accompanied by a standard hibiscus underplanted with petunias.

CHAPTER 4

Containers on the Patio and Balcony

Whether a patio is a small courtyard, a raised terrace or the entire backyard of a townhouse garden, it is usually an area where lawn has been replaced by paving, a wooden deck or pebbles, and trees, shrubs, annuals and other plants are grown in confined spaces. For this reason containers can be used to maximum effect.

A group of soft pink azaleas creates a charming picture in a corner of a small patio.

Opposite: Campanulas, begonias and impatiens in square concrete containers relish the cool, damp conditions in a cool, shady corner of a paved patio.

Design

A patio is usually an extension of the house and forms a link between house and garden – so it works best to keep to the style and colouring of the house when buying and placing the containers. The same applies to a balcony, which is also an inherent part of the home – make sure that the colours, shapes and plants that you choose harmonize with your home. When selecting pots and plants, you should also give some thought to the patio or balcony furniture – their style, size and colour. Then sit back and imagine the plants to be used.

Whereas a patio may lead onto the garden, and is usually at ground level, a balcony may be far above ground level, forming a small, self-con-

tained world of growing things. It is vital that every container and every plant counts in the overall plan, where scale and proportion are of extreme importance. For instance, a group of round, fat containers will take up a great deal of space, which is at a premium on a small balcony, while one or two tall, slender jars overlooking a shallow dish will be much more pleasing. A shelf, or a low table, pushed against a wall, can hold several containers, and provide useful storage space underneath.

Available space

On a patio with plenty of space, large containers can be most striking – wooden wine barrels or large terracotta pots planted with large plants such as citrus trees, ficus trees, acers, camellias and hydrangeas, underplanted with brightly flowering annuals. You can create the effect of an entire garden on your patio by grouping a variety of plants and containers of different sizes and shapes and adding interesting ornaments for variety or focal points. Container-grown plants on the patio can even provide shade. On a small patio, two slender conifers, such as "Sky Rocket", will be much more suitable than rounded shrubs with dense foliage, such as syzygium.

A patio or balcony with lots of containers dotted around may look and feel crowded – your plants may be displayed with far greater effect if

you group your containers in one or two corners. Also make use of shelves, hanging baskets and windowboxes to exploit all the available space.

Perspective

Attention must be given to perspective in the overall design of your patio or balcony. To make a balcony or patio appear longer, place plants with small or feathery leaves at the far end, and larger ones closer to the viewer. Colour can also bring about this effect by placing subtle colours at the far end and brighter colours closer. And, of course, the opposite applies if there is a need to make the view seem shorter.

Colour

In a confined space, colour counts, and it is good to lay down a foundation of foliage, choosing from a selection of greens and greys, or variegated foliage, and of different textures, for permanent interest.

The entire patio can be framed with evergreen climbers to form a permanent backdrop for colourful seasonal flowers. A measure of constraint is necessary, however, to avoid a crowded and cluttered look.

A wooden bench and an interesting collection of container plants create a quiet sitting-out area on a balcony.

Opposite: The superb condition of the begonias, hydrangeas, fuchsias, cordyline and other container plants brings a touch of luxury to this patio, where the sound of water adds to the tranquillity.

Practical Considerations

Container plants should enhance the patio or balcony and not interfere with its function as a sitting-out area. This has some practical implications.

Waste water

An important factor that must be considered for container plants on the patio or balcony is the need for the disposal of waste water, which cannot be allowed to run onto the floor surface. One method is to lay down a good layer of gravel or stones in the bottom of the container, then to water the plant carefully so that it does not become waterlogged.

Most containers are available with a drip tray to collect surplus water. Placing ready-planted pots within larger containers with drainage material in their base will also deal with the problem. Very useful for these conditions are self-watering containers. Hanging baskets will drip after being watered, which should be provided for.

Weight

Weight, too, is a consideration on a suspended balcony. A large container filled with soil can be extremely heavy and could be a danger. For this reason lightweight containers made of polystyrene or compressed cellulose may be more suitable on a balcony. If you live in a flat, it may be necessary to obtain permission to place containers on your balcony.

Positioning of containers

When you select container-grown plants suitable for shade or sun, bear in mind that the sun moves from east to west. In winter, a north-facing, sunny patio or balcony is a boon in the mornings, whereas when the sun comes west, shade is appreciated in at least part of the area. Place your containers in such a way that the plants will obtain the maximum benefit from the micro-climate.

If wind is a problem, use a trellis, a frame of glass, or even wind-resistant container plants to provide shelter. Patios and balconies are places of entertainment or at the very least of sitting out and relaxing, so make sure plants are not going to be damaged by passing traffic. Rather place them where they may be seen, admired and enjoyed. Also, prickly or thorny plants should be avoided, and if there will be children around, make sure that you don't have any plants which bear poisonous berries, flowers or leaves.

Choice of Containers

In a confined space, it is usually better to keep to one type of material or colour for containers, although a good effect may be achieved by placing one very large round pot planted with dramatic plants, and surrounding it with smaller containers perhaps of a different texture.

A combination of pots, troughs and hanging baskets will create a pleasant, lush environment. Round containers are easy to plant with a selection of plants – a tall standard in the centre can have lower-growing or cascading plants at its feet. Square containers will need to be softened by tumbling plants, and long, narrow containers and windowboxes are better placed on a windowsill, or against a wall or balcony railing. To bring height and add interest to the grouping, place some containers onto sleepers or other platforms or pedestals.

A healthy fern, a tree begonia, hostas and hydrangeas nestle in a shady corner.

Strawberry pots (containers with several openings in their sides) are very useful in confined spaces, and look lovely on the patio when planted heavily with annuals or bulbs. Herbs will also grow well in them, as well as the strawberries for which they were originally intended.

Painting your containers to match the windowframes, doors or the upholstery of the home has attractive results. A contrast of colours could also look striking. It is not difficult to paint containers, and plastic or fibre-cement containers can easily be turned into part of the decor (*see* p.24).

Finishing Touches

Pebbles can bring about a sense of the outdoors and detract from an unattractive floor covering, if necessary. Concrete birds and animals can add a lovely finishing touch, although this should never be overdone.

Lighting on the patio need not only be functional, but may be used to complement or highlight selected elements of your patio garden. Aluminium wall lights, a cast aluminium pedestal light or even a stone Japanese lantern will form an attractive focal point surrounded with plant-filled containers.

Try using a mirror mounted to a wall among a group of containers to create an illusion of space, or to reflect a particularly attractive plant or group of plants. Special care must be taken to provide a waterproof backing, and if the mirror is framed, make sure that the frame consists of a waterproof material.

A single pedestal with an urn, an alcove in the wall, or even a small statue placed in the distance, can act as a focal point on the patio, bringing together a group of container-grown plants.

PLANTING A WATER LILY

A large container of suitable depth (it should be least 45 cm deep) can be host to a single water lily. If there are fish in the container, the lily should be allowed to cover only two thirds of the water surface. Plant the water lily into a plastic pot filled with compost or rich soil, place pebbles on the soil surface and hold them down with wire netting. Then lower the pot carefully into the larger container.

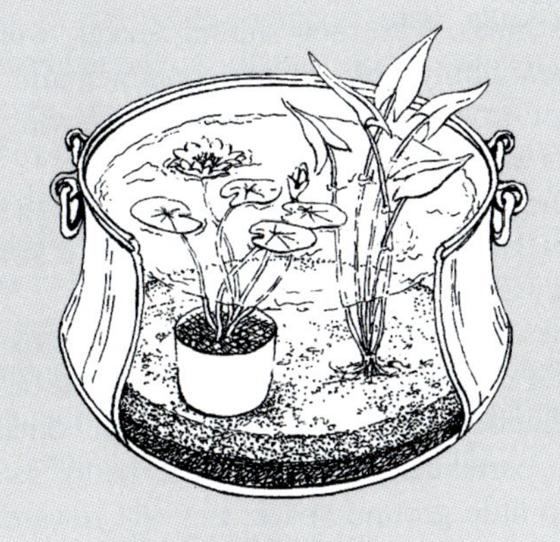

WATER FEATURES

Just one pretty shallow dish of water on the patio will immediately create an atmosphere of tranquillity as well as bringing reflections.

Oxygenating plants such as vallisneria and elodea, which can be planted in the same way as a water lily, will keep the fish happy. On the market now is a large range of do-it-yourself water features. Some have a natural, earthy look and are equally suitable for the garden, the patio or a balcony. Others, of ceramic, have to be sheltered from the elements. All are easy to install.

OTHER STRUCTURES

A trellis of wood or iron is not only decorative, but may be put to good use as support for climbers, or to divide off part of the patio. The trellis can be either free standing, or attached to a patio wall.

A large, open patio may be enhanced by the addition of a pergola, and there are many climbers which can be planted in large containers and trained to cover the pergola.

A pergola covered with a climber such as wisteria can give you the best of both worlds on your patio – shade in summer, but letting in the sunlight in winter after having dropped its leaves in autumn.

PLANNING THE PLANTING

There is a vast range of plants to choose from, but careful planning is essential. Bear in mind the special use of plants – for shade or sun, upright or cascading, flowering or foliage, possibly as a windbreak. You will need background plants, accent plants, a good mix of different shapes and sizes, and a selection of annuals and perennials to knit them all together.

In the sunnier parts, brightly coloured flowers may be the order of the day, either in annual or permanent form. Combine shrubs, perennials and annuals available, in colours which you would like to bring together. Shapes may be many and varied, from tall and slender, such as

Old pillars and decorative iron-work match the country look of the patio, the scarlet and mauve petunias forming a bold contrast with the more delicate colour of the primulas.

"Stargazers" are among the many liliums suited to container planting, making a spectacular show in summer. They need excellent drainage.

CHAPTER 5

Colour from Flowers and Foliage

Opposite: Dutch irises, tall and slender, can be planted as close as 6 cm apart. English daisies act as a groundcover.

Hyacinth bulbs (below) should be planted just under the surface of the soil which should be organically enriched.

Many flowering and foliage plants are eminently suitable for planting in containers. Annuals, as the name suggests, come to maturity, bloom and set seed in one season, and are then discarded to make way for others. Perennials, on the other hand, are permanent residents, and should be carefully chosen to make sure they look good even when they are not in flower. Flowering plants that are only good-looking while in flower, such as spring and winter bulbs, can be planted in containers and then moved about, or lifted and replanted in the garden until blooming time comes round again.

It is not always the flowers that bring welcome colour. Many plants – annual and perennial – also have beautiful, coloured foliage. These may make a statement on their own, or they will blend or contrast with flowering plants.

Colour All Year Round

With careful planning, and making the best use of seasonal annuals and bulbs and the more permanent perennials, interplanted with foliage plants chosen for their colour and texture, you can have colour in your containers all year round.

Mixing flowering annuals with winter and spring bulbs means that when they have finished flowering, they can be taken out immediately and the bulbs placed elsewhere. Then come the summer bloomers – bulbs, annuals or perennials – which will fill your containers to overflowing.

Add to this a variety of foliage plants, chosen for seasonal colour or permanent texture, to contrast or harmonize with flowering plants.

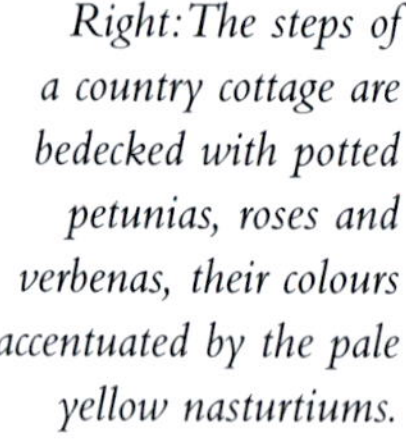

Right: The steps of a country cottage are bedecked with potted petunias, roses and verbenas, their colours accentuated by the pale yellow nasturtiums.

Far right: The bold shape of the dark green bergenia leaves show up the delicate beauty of primulas and impatiens.

Below: A happy profusion of pansies in a variety of colours.

Flowering Annuals

Seedlings for flowering annuals are often available at the point of blooming, which saves a lot of time, and helps to keep containers constantly brimming with colour.

Annuals have different growth forms which may differ even within the same species. Lobelias may form compact cushions or cascading curtains of delicate blue or white flowers, depending on the variety you choose.

Petunias, too, may spread or tumble, or form mounds of colour. By choosing cleverly, you can, therefore, have upright plants in the middle of a container, with other forms of the same plant tumbling over the edge.

General growing conditions

The main planting times for annuals are spring and autumn, but by careful selection, and relentlessly taking out the plants when they have finished blooming, a succession of blooms in containers is possible throughout spring and summer, and even well into autumn. Annuals generally come to their best in full sun, some of the lovely exceptions being impatiens, begonias and torenias. They must have well-drained soil, and most of them should not be given too much nitrogen, which will result in too many leaves at the expense of flowers.

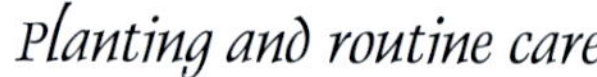

Planting and routine care

Make sure the drainage holes are covered with crocks or stones to allow for drainage, then fill the container with good garden soil or a commercial potting mix to which a slow-release potplant fertilizer has been added.

Water the soil to allow it to settle, so the soil level is about 3 cm below the lip of the container, then plant the seedlings or small plants. For a good show of colour, the distance between plants should be less than in beds.

Keep the seedlings damp until the plants are well established, then water deeply twice a week, or more during very dry periods, bearing in mind that containers dry out more quickly than soil in the garden.

Deadheading is probably the most important chore in the care of annuals. Annuals will not only bloom for a longer period if dead flowers are removed, they will also remain neat.

Dead leaves should also be removed regularly, as should any straggling stems which have no flowers on them.

• Annuals for Containers •

Alyssum *(Lobularia maritima)* is a most obliging plant, bearing flowers of pink-mauve or glistening white. Alyssum grows well in full sun or light shade, and will mix well with any other plants. Plant it with petunias, lobelias, ivy-leafed pelargoniums or pansies, or underplant ranunculi, freesias and sparaxis. If alyssum seedlings are inserted in slits in the side of a hanging basket, they will soon cascade in curtains of flowers. Plant a row of white alyssum along the edge of a windowbox, then plant white Dutch irises close together in the centre, underplanted with blue muscari, and plant "Ice Follies" daffodils at the back.

Begonias *(Begonia semperflorens)* do equally well in full sun or semi-shade. The pink or white flowers form cushions of colour from late spring to autumn. They will not take heavy frost but will last into the next season if they are lifted and planted into bags in a sheltered place. Plant pink and white together, and give them an edging of blue myosotis (forget-me-not), or cascading blue lobelias. They will also provide a colourful, compact groundcover under tall-growing trees and shrubs.

Cineraria *(Senecio cruentus)* come in many glamorous colours and look good in containers, but will not take frost, so should be placed on a sheltered balcony or patio. They need loose, friable soil, plenty of water, and additional food during their growing season. Although they are lovely on their own, a sprinkling of alyssum between them will show up their vibrant colours.

Forget-me-not *(Myosotis alpestris)* grows in the shade or semi-shade, and has a low growth making it a suitable edging plant. With its small, vivid blue flowers, myosotis will make a pretty picture planted among Dutch irises or daffodils in a fairly shallow container. Ferns and myosotis planted with fuchsias will bring about a cool effect.

Impatiens *(Impatiens walleriana)*, the well-loved busy lizzies, will grow in shade or semi-shade, and provided they are well watered, even tolerate full sun for most of the day except the hot afternoon sun. The compact varieties are ideal for containers and hanging baskets, and are available in separate colours ranging from purple and scarlet to pink and white. There are also varieties with variegated leaves and extra-large flowers. Plant impatiens in the shade with ferns and other foliage plants such as aspidistras, and in warmer areas with dieffenbachias and ctenanthes. They will also make a good groundcover with a large potted ficus. Impatiens and hydrangeas are both summer bloomers and will make a good combination.

Lobelias *(Lobelia erinus)* are sun lovers and among the best plants for containers and baskets; they have a long blooming season as they come into bloom when the plants are quite small. Blue or white, they mix easily with other annuals such as petunias and primulas, and will grow willingly among bulbs such as daffodils and tulips, or perennials such as pelargoniums.

The colours of impatiens are many and varied. Here, pink and crimson have been planted among lavender and rosemary.

Marigolds *(Tagetes spp.).* Many gardeners are put off by what is regarded as the harsh oranges in marigolds, but they also come in pale lemon and yellow, which, with their upright growth, make them ideal for the centre of a container. They prefer full sun, and seed can be sown in the container. Mix marigolds with alyssum and pale blue lobelias, or torenias.

Nasturtiums *(Tropaeolum spp.).* The newer varieties have a more compact growth than the older ones which were inclined to rampant growth and getting out of hand. Place them in a sunny position and pinch back the early growth several times to ensure bushy growth. Try planting nasturtiums in a tall Aladdin pot and let them cascade to the ground. They should not be overfed or over-watered, to encourage the plants to produce more flowers, which come in shades of bright yellow, orange and red.

Nicotiana *(Nicotiana alata).* It is certainly worthwhile growing at least a few nicotiana (also called tobacco flowers) in containers on the patio or balcony, not only for their sweet evening perfume, but also for their clusters of red, pink or white flowers. Particularly attractive is the Tinkerbell series – dwarf growing, with a multitude of flowers.

Petunia "California Girl" is a prolific bloomer and regular dead-heading will result in a long flowering season.

Pansies *(Viola x wittrockiana),* with their showy, velvety flowers, are surely among the most popular of annuals, and the selection of colours grows annually. A few pansies in a small pot are a delight, and planted more generously, they will make a splendid show in winter and spring, often blooming well into the hot summer months. They do equally well in full sun or semi-shade. Pansies make a spectacular show on their own if you use different shades – all pink, all blue or all yellow – but they also mix happily with other annuals such as cinerarias, or planted among daffodils, freesias and tulips. Surround a central planting of *Begonia semperflorens* with vivid blue pansies and pink alyssum.

Petunias *(Petunia spp.)* on the whole, are sun-lovers and do not take kindly to rainy weather, which means that in the summer rainfall areas they are at their best in the dry winter months, and in the Western Cape they do better in the dry summer months. The early growth can be pinched back for a compact, bushy form. With the vast range of colours, flower size and growth forms available, it is possible to have a festival of petunias on the patio, planted in baskets, window-boxes and containers. Petunias mix well with other annuals such as lobelias, nemesias and alyssum. Mix pink or purple cascading petunias with grey foliage plants, such as artemisia, or give a standard fuchsia a gay accompaniment of petunias. The new "Surfinia" petunias have long stems of up to 1 m, making them ideal for baskets and urns, or trailing from the edge of a windowbox where they can contrast with the upright growth of lavenders or dwarf conifers.

Primulas *(Primula spp.).* Most popular among the primulas is *P. malacoides,* a true annual. In troughs and low containers, planted close together, they will create a gentle mist of colour, from pink, mauve and purple, to white. Pure white primulas will look lovely under tall blue Dutch irises, with blue and white petunias trailing over the edge of the container. *P. obconi-*

ca, in shades of blue, pink, orange and white, has round leaves and rounded flower heads. They are taller than *P. malacoides* and can be planted in the centre of a container, surrounded by small ferns, pansies, violas, alyssum or trailing lobelias. Cut back the flowered stems to ground level to encourage further blooming. They do best in shade or semi-shade.

Sweet peas *(Lathyrus odoratus)*. The "Bijous", "Kneehi's" and "Little Sweethearts" are fast-growing dwarf-bush varieties and make excellent container subjects. They can be persuaded to climb up wigwams of sticks placed in a container, with cascading pelargoniums planted at the edge, or they can cascade over the edge of a container planted with fuchsias, lavender or winter bulbs such as Dutch irises and daffodils. These sweet-smelling sun lovers need well-prepared soil. They come in a wide variety of colours and provide excellent cut flowers so you can enjoy their fragrance in the house too. Most common are the winter-flowering varieties, but summer-flowering varieties can be grown in colder parts of the country.

Torenias *(Torenia fournieri)*. These summer-flowering annuals, also known as wishbone flowers, are now available not only in the well-known blue, but also in shades of pink and mauve. They prefer rich, well-drained soil and a moist, semi-shaded position. They have an upright, slender growth, ideal for planting in the centre of a container with an edging of alyssum or lobelia. For a startling effect, mix torenias and yellow marigolds in the centre of a container and give them an edging of white alyssum and lilac petunias.

Verbenas *(Verbena spp.)* may be brilliant red or purple, but they also come in softer shades of pink and mauve. They are low-growing, generous bloomers, and will need space to spread their stems bearing the flowers. Mix mauve verbenas with lavender or felicia, or for a truly sumptuous effect, allow scarlet verbenas to overflow a container planted with violet heliotrope. Verbenas do best in a sunny position.

A tumbling of mauve sweet peas blends well with the pink daisies and azaleas in the shaded bed in the background.
Below left: Violas of clear gold in a dark green painted pot, beautifully offsetting their colour, herald the coming of spring.

Violas *(Viola spp.)* are available in separate, clear colours, from white through yellow to blue and purple, and are ideal for creating a specific colour scheme. Think of blue violas with yellow daffodils, or yellow violas with blue lobelias or torenias, or a hanging basket of blue and yellow violas with cascading white petunias. "Prince Henry", a small flower of deep purple, flowers freely, and will happily cascade from a basket. Try planting a mound of *Begonia semperflorens*, with "Prince Henry" around the edge of the container. Fill containers with compost-rich soil before planting violas and place them in a semi-shaded position for the best results.

Flowering Perennials

Flowering perennials produce flowers annually during a specific season, and a careful selection of perennials for each season will ensure colour in your containers all year round. Evergreen perennials, such as dianthus, do not lose their foliage after the flowering period, while most herbaceous perennials are deciduous and die down completely after blooming.

General growing conditions

Most perennials are easy to care for, provided you grow them in a suitable position in well-drained soil (*also see* plant discussions). Many perennials are quite happy to stay in their containers for several years before being divided and replanted. After division, perennials should be replanted into new, enriched soil.

After flowering, deciduous perennials can be moved, pot and all, to a place where they may enjoy a good rest. The evergreens can be left after flowering to present their foliage, possibly with the company of flowering annuals.

Planting and routine care

Most of the popular and easy to grow perennials are available from nurseries in pots, some already in flower, and can be planted straight into the container you have selected for them. Although most perennials do better planted on their own and allowed to fill their pot, some can be given the company of annuals during their flowering season. It is not a good idea to plant annuals with perennials which are about to die down, as this will not only bring about an untidy appearance, but the dormant rootstock might suffer from the extra food and water given to the annuals.

Yellow chrysanthemums and marigolds in a shallow container have been set in a sea of blue browallias for late summer colour.

• Perennials for Containers •

Above: A large, ornate urn generously planted with brachycome, lobelia, scaevola and petunias dominates its lower neighbours in this shady spot of the garden.
Left: Dianthus will quickly spread its roots throughout a pot and should be divided every year or two.

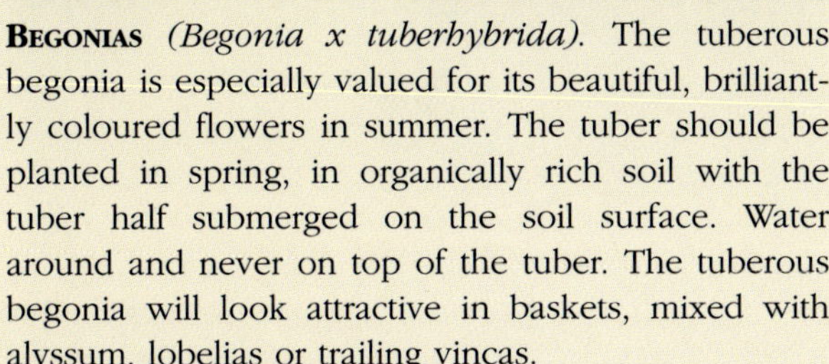

Begonias *(Begonia x tuberhybrida).* The tuberous begonia is especially valued for its beautiful, brilliantly coloured flowers in summer. The tuber should be planted in spring, in organically rich soil with the tuber half submerged on the soil surface. Water around and never on top of the tuber. The tuberous begonia will look attractive in baskets, mixed with alyssum, lobelias or trailing vincas.

Bromeliads (various genera) come from the steamy tropics and need warmth and moisture to keep them healthy. They vary between the fine, lacy growth of the Spanish moss, to the gigantic pineapple bromeliads. Tank bromeliads should have their tanks filled with water, and, as with other terrestrials, must have an extremely well-drained growing medium, helped by the addition of charcoal, stones and coarse sand. Watering must be thorough, but cut down in winter. Epiphytes, including the tillandsias, need little water, except for the spraying of leaves. Bromeliads will give a permanent, spectacular display, but it is advisable to consult your nursery before investing in these plants.

Campanulas *(Campanula spp.).* The taller-growing campanulas are not well suited to container planting, but *C. carpatica* (bellflower) is evergreen and will show off its dark-green, toothed leaves, then bloom from spring through summer. The attractive, bell-shaped flowers come in blue or white. It is inclined to form a thick mat of roots and is generally not a good mixer, tending to stifle its companions. However, it will look good planted as a groundcover under a standard syzygium or a standard fuchsia in a good-sized container, provided that it is kept in check. They do best in shade or semi-shade in a sheltered position, and need plenty of water.

Dianthus *(Dianthus x alwoodii).* With their sweet-smelling flowers and vivid colours, ranging from pink to crimson, dianthus, also known as pinks, will make a happy addition to any container planting. Place these quick-growing perennials in a sunny position and they will reward you with bright flowers from early summer through autumn. Combine them with pink alyssum, blue lobelias, and blue and white Dutch irises. After blooming, the plants can be removed from the container and planted in the garden to be brought into new growth for the following season.

Felicias *(Felicia amelloides).* Perennial felicias may become a bit straggly, but if clipped back regularly when young, they will form a compact, low-growing bush covered in blue or mauve, daisy-like flowers with yellow centres. They are suitable for underplanting trees and tall-growing shrubs and will willingly tumble over the side of a container. These indigenous plants flower in summer and need a sunny position.

Gazanias *(Gazania spp.).* For that hot, sunny part of the garden or patio, gazanias will bring splashes of brilliant colour – orange, bronze, bright yellow and pink – from spring through summer and autumn. Some hybrids bear flowers of pale yellow. After flowering, plants will become untidy. Gazania clumps can be divided, taking the outer growth for replanting, or take cuttings, which will provide vigorous new plants. Their vivid colours make them ideal companions for dimorphotheca, and they contrast well with felicias.

Hellebores *(Helleborus spp.).* These herbaceous perennials are becoming more freely available and look pretty in a container, but as they die down almost completely in autumn, they will have a period of non-productivity. Nevertheless, they are well worthwhile in colder climates and some varieties *(H. argutifolius* and *H. niger)* are actually renowned for their winter appeal, both from their leathery dark green leaves and their white, cup-shaped flowers which are suitable for cutting. Place their containers in semi-shade and water them frequently.

Just one marguerite plant was sufficient to fill this pot to overflowing. The early growth was pinched back, to ensure a compact and bushy form.

Marguerites *(Argyranthemum frutescens).* These easy growing perennials are also known as the daisy bush, bearing single or double flowers in a variety of colours. Plant one healthy plant to a pot, pinch back the early growth to encourage a bushy form and give it an extra boost of fertilizer as it comes into full growth to support the plant which is normally large relative to the size of the pot. Take cuttings constantly to keep up a supply of healthy plants and remove dead flowerheads to extend the blooming period. Place their containers in a sunny position and fill with fertile soil.

Pelargoniums – *see* p. 100

Periwinkle *(Vinca spp.).* This trailing, evergreen perennial spreads its slender stems over the edge of a container, and bears its blue or white open-faced flowers generously, and is ideal for trailing from a windowbox or basket. Mix vinca with cascading fuchsias, maidenhair fern, impatiens and myosotis in a shady windowbox, or, for a sunnier position, let it trail from a basket with petunias, *Begonia semperflorens* and alyssum. It will make a good groundcover for azaleas or hydrangeas. Mix it with ivy and chlorophytum for an all-foliage combination, or plant a tall urn with a bronze cordyline and allow the vinca to tumble over the edge. Vinca grows well in full sun or semi-shade, and needs well-drained, compost-rich soil and frequent watering.

Bulbs and Similar Plants

Spring and winter bulbs are an annual delight, and are highly suited to container planting. A variety of bulbs blooms in summer as well. Several bulbs of varying heights and colours can be grouped together in a trough or half-barrel for a spectacular display on the patio. A combination of bulbs and seasonal annuals in the same container also makes a particularly attractive display. When planting bulbs in windowboxes, use the smaller or dwarf varieties around the edge, and normal sized plants in the centre to lend height.

General growing conditions

The term "bulbs" covers the true bulbs such as daffodils and hyacinths, as well as corms, tubers and fleshy roots, and the same general growing conditions apply.

The biggest advantages of planting bulbs into containers are that their growing conditions can be controlled and that they are free from the attacks of moles. They can also be given a rest after dying down, and need not cope with the heavy watering of plants around them.

Planting and routine care

April is the best time to plant winter and spring bulbs, except for tulips which are better kept for May planting. Summer-blooming bulbs are usually planted, or brought into new growth, in spring. Most bulbs like a sunny, or semi-shaded, well-drained position and thrive in well-enriched soil. Bulbs are usually planted up to two or three times their depth, in other words, if a daffodil bulb measures 5 cm from top to bottom, it is planted at a depth of 15 cm.

The soil in containers must be extremely well drained for the planting of bulbs, as waterlogged conditions will surely cause them to rot. Before planting, dust them with fungicide, then plant them into a bed of clean sand.

From planting time, they must be kept moist at all times, the watering being deep enough to reach right down to the roots – a good soaking two or three times a week is better than mere sprinklings every day. As the leaves become well formed, they will benefit from weak liquid manure every ten days, followed by a thorough soaking. Evergreen plants may be lifted and divided after blooming, and replanted into replenished soil, but those whose leaves die down should be left until the leaves have died down completely, while you keep up the watering.

Above: Hellebores, lobelias and pelargoniums are a good combination in a concrete pot placed in a mixed bed.

Left: Narcissus and primulas planted in a wide, shallow container make a spectacular show in early spring.

Opposite top: Bromeliads have highly coloured leaves and eye-catching flowers, some of them in highly unusual combinations of colour, such as tillandsias with their flowers of purple and shocking pink.

· Winter & Spring Bulbs for Containers ·

Alliums *(Allium neapolitanum)*. The garlic chive, with its white umbrellas of star-shaped flowers on slender stems, is suited for planting in the centre of a container. Mix them with white or pink alyssum, blue lobelias, blue muscari or blue pansies.

Anemones *(Anemone coronaria)*. The single or double flowers of anemones have vibrant colours and make a lovely display on their own in a tub-like container. The "St Brigid" and "De Caen" series have particularly vivid colours which will be shown up by the blue of myosotis or lobelia, planted as an edging. Try mixing anemones with daffodils and other bulbs, such as blue and white Dutch irises with an edging of alyssum or yellow violas.

Babiana *(Babiana stricta)* with their blue and purple flowers, dark green, pleated leaves and sturdy stems make happy container plants and are good mixers, especially with muscari in a small pot. They will also go well with freesias and sparaxis with a touch of blue lobelias. They need a sunny or semi-shaded position and well-drained soil with a sprinkling of bone meal at planting.

Chinkerinchees *(Ornithogalum thyrsoides)*. These indigenous bulbs with their striking, white flowers grow rather tall for smaller containers, but planted *en masse* in a trough or large container placed at ground level, they will make an attractive display and provide excellent cut flowers for the home.

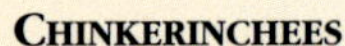

If tall-growing hyacinths need to be staked, slender sticks should be used so as not to be too obtrusive.

Clivias *(Clivia spp.)* thrive in the rich leafmould of our indigenous forests, and so need a shady position and rich, friable soil. *C. miniata* is the best known, with its orange tubular flowers and dark green strap-like leaves. There is also a yellow variety. They make good container subjects for the shady part of the patio, or try placing one or two containers filled with clivias under tall tree ferns or along a shady path.

Daffodils *(Narcissus spp.)* come in a wide range of shapes and sizes in various shades of yellow and cream, including two-colour combinations. The dwarf varieties are particularly suited to container planting. Plant them 5 cm apart and never let them dry out from the time they are planted. Give them a carpet of purple alyssum or plant them among nemesias in a windowbox, and allow freesias to flow over the edge. If you have acers planted in a fairly large container, give them a carpet of daffodils for a woodland effect. In the semi-shade, plant muscari among the daffodils, with a border of lachenalia. Mix daffodils, Dutch irises, ranunculi and anemones in a large tub for a spring spectacle. Daffodils will need liquid manure to bring them to their best. Continue watering daffodils after the flowering period until the last leaf has died down to ensure that all the goodness in the soil has gone into the bulb for the next season.

Freesias *(Freesia refracta)*. Plant freesias in containers close to the house so that you can enjoy their lovely, bright colours and heavy fragrance. They are inclined to straggle, and are best planted around the edge of a large container or windowbox. The windowbox can be planted with a mass of *Primula malacoides* interspersed with daffodils, or more permanent residents such as lavender. Or try planting trailing mauve verbenas which will combine beautifully with the freesias.

Grape hyacinths *(Muscari spp.)* have narrow leaves from which arise short stems bearing tiny, fragrant, blue bells. They are lovely for mixing with other bulbs and annuals. For a bright springtime display in a shaded or semi-shaded position, combine them with yellow primulas and pale blue irises.

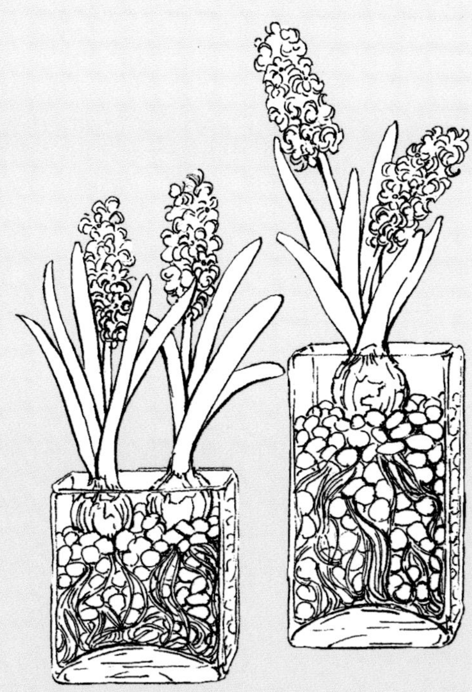

Hyacinths *(Hyacinthus spp.)* are glamorous indeed, with their spires of sweet-scented flowers. They are fine in low troughs, or pretty dishes on the patio. They will grow in soil, but may also sit on pebbles at water level. Fill a glass bowl with pebbles or glass marbles, cover the pebbles or marbles with water and "sit" the hyacinth bulbs on them so that just their lower surface is touching the water (it may be necessary to balance the bulb with pebbles or marbles). The bulbs will soon sprout roots, followed by leaves and flowers (*see* illustration above). As such bulbs will not survive until the following season, they can be discarded after blooming. Hyacinths can be encouraged into growth ("forced") by filling a glass container with water and sitting the bulb on the surface – the use of glass marbles will ensure that the bulb sits straight. Now place it in a dark cupboard, bring it out when a good root system has developed, and watch the flowers develop.

Ifafa lilies *(Cyrtanthus mackenii)* take well to planting in containers and are wind tolerant. The indigenous ifafa lily has small, tubular yellow flowers, while some hybrids have flowers of pink and apricot. They take a little time to recover from transplanting, and are best left until the clumps are overcrowded. Plant them into a large, shallow bowl, and give them lobelias or alyssum for company. Allow them to die down comfortably after flowering during spring and early summer, then when they come into new growth, watch out for caterpillars which often get right down into the plant, and deal with them immediately.

Iris *(Iris spp.)*. Dutch irises are the only irises which are really suited to container planting. They come in blue, white, yellow or purple and can be planted 6 cm apart. Plant them in a trough with hyacinths or daffodils, or combine all three, with muscari planted around the edge.

Lachenalias *(Lachenalia spp.)* are low growing, some having purple-speckled leaves. With their spikes of bell-shaped flowers in yellow or coral red, they look particularly attractive around the edge of a container. *L. viridiflora* has green flowers and will look spectacular around the edge of a container filled with daffodils or irises interplanted with lobelia or alyssum. They prefer full sun and are best displayed planted closely together. Lachenalias are frost tender and need well-drained soil.

Ranunculi *(Ranunculus asiaticus)* are greedy feeders, and must have well-dug, well-enriched soil. Plant them close together in a large container sheltered from the wind, and give them the company of blue lobelias for the best display of their colourful double blooms.

Sparaxis *(Sparaxis spp.)*. Also known as harlequin flowers, sparaxis must have full sun and extremely well-drained soil. Allow them to fill a container on their own, then lift them when they have died down and keep the bulbs in a cool, dry place until autumn.

Spring snowflake *(Leucojum vernum)*. One of the few bulbs that do well in a shady position, spring snowflake produces a lot of dark green, strap-like leaves and delicate, white, bell-shaped flowers. Leucojum have a rather untidy habit of straggling leaves and are best planted *en masse* in their own large container where they can grow unfettered and show off their pretty flowers. However, they can be grown in a large container under a large tree. They will not do well in very hot, dry regions, and their soil must be moist at all times during the growing season.

Tulips *(Tulipa spp.).* A wide range of treated tulips, which bloom very well, are available in almost any colour imaginable. Tulips should be planted only in May, away from any reflected light from paths or walls, in well-drained soil heavily enriched with well-rotted compost and manure. Tulips make such an impact on their own that many gardeners prefer to plant them unaccompanied by other plants, but there is no doubt that they will be shown up by the addition of subtly coloured pansies and violas. For a richly coloured cameo, surround them with *Primula veris.*

For a splendid show in spring, plant tulips close together in well-enriched, well-drained soil, and feed them with regular applications of water and weak liquid manure.

• Summer Bulbs for Containers •

Agapanthus *(Agapanthus spp.)* are not usually seen in containers in this country, although dwarf agapanthus of blue or white with their upright growth make a striking display on their own in terracotta pots, or bring about a woodland effect if planted with taller trees. They will grow in sun or shade in well-drained soil.

Amazon lilies *(Eucharis grandiflora)* have fragrant white flowers and should be given plenty of space, such as wine barrels or large containers, in which to grow undisturbed. They need rich, well-drained soil and plenty of water during the growing season, with the addition of weak liquid manure every ten days. As they prefer shade or semi-shade, they can be given the company of ferns or impatiens.

Berg lilies *(Galtonia candicans).* Also known as Cape hyacinth, berg lilies send up tall slender stems bearing fragrant white bell-flowers in summer. In their natural habitat, they form communities of plants in sunny, wind-protected spots. They must have well-drained soil and a lot of water during the growing season. Dwarf blue agapanthus will be good companions for berg lilies.

Crinums *(Crinum spp.),* whose flowers range from white to pink, depending on the species, have broad strap-like leaves. They are very prone to the amaryllis caterpillar which can be dealt with in the early stages with a good insecticide. They do best planted on their own in a container.

Gladioli *(Gladiolus spp.)* make a splendid show of blooms, but look untidy once the flowers are finished. Planted in containers, they can be placed among other flowers in a wind-sheltered, sunny position, and when the flowering period is over, the entire container can be moved to allow the leaves to die down. Gladioli take 90 days to flower from planting. Plant the bulbs 10 cm apart, and give each bulb a teaspoon of bone meal at planting.

Lilies *(Lilium spp.).* From the lower growing Asiatic hybrids to the tall trumpets and oriental hybrids, liliums with their large flowers look superb in containers. Their most important growing requirements are extremely well-drained soil and plenty of well-rotted organics. Containers should be large and deep enough to accommodate the spread and depth of the roots. Buy or plant bulbs in autumn or spring, keep them damp until they are in full growth, then give them plenty of water, and liquid manure.

Pineapple flower *(Eucomis autumnalis)* is an indigenous plant with wide strap leaves and heads of small flowers borne around a tall stem with a rosette of green leaves at the top, rather resembling a pineapple. It is inclined to straggle and should be given support. Plant several pineapple flowers in a wide container and allow ivies or vinca to tumble over the edge.

Spider lily *(Hymenocallis littoralis)* has strange flowers of white and pale green with loose segments resembling spiders' legs, and always evokes interest when it is in flower. It does best in shade or semi-shade. Plant these lilies in a large container in a sheltered corner of the patio and ensure that the flowers are easily visible. A darker green background of maidenhair or leather fern will add more interest and offset the flowers.

Overleaf: Ranunculi are heavy feeders, but it is well worthwhile giving them every attention to ensure a profusion of vibrantly coloured flowers.

Left: The sturdy, slender stems of summer-blooming crinum flowers rise from their dark green strap-like leaves.

The white flowers of Lilium auratum and the pink "Stargazer" combined with the neighbouring penstemmons create a gay picture of summer beauty.

Foliage Plants

Foliage plants are of great importance in containers, as they can form the backdrop for more colourful flowering plants. Many also come into their own for their colour and texture. Several foliage plants with contrasting colours and shapes may be grouped together in one container for permanent or seasonal interest. Often foliage plants are grown in containers mainly for their foliage to contrast or harmonize with brightly flowering annuals. By filling a dark corner of the patio with variegated foliage plants with light and bright yellow stripes or specks you can create the illusion of dappled sunlight.

There are many leafy subjects to be considered for container planting – from the small annual coleus to the philodendron with its giant leaves (*see* p.77). Leaves of many sizes, shapes and textures, and plants of different growth forms give you an almost endless choice. Probably the most important among the foliage plants are the grey-leafed plants, including *Senecio maritima*, *Artemisia spp.*, *Stachys byzantina* (lamb's ear) and *Santolina chamaecyparissus* (lavender cotton), which may either blend beautifully with other colours, or tone down harsh or over-bright colours. The following selection is mainly annuals and perennials. (For shrubs and trees, *see* p. 68, and for cacti and other succulents, p. 80.)

• Foliage Plants for Containers •

Aglaonema *(Aglaonema spp.)* will not take frost, but in subtropical gardens it makes a splendid container plant for placing on the patio, or in shady parts of the garden. With its handsome broad leaves of green and variegations, it resembles a dieffenbachia and is a valued foliage plant. It needs plenty of water at all times and must be protected from the wind.

Ajuga *(Ajuga reptans)* has a neat appearance, its leaves growing close to the ground, forming a compact mat. "Burgundy lace" has leaves variegated in pink and cream, and will go well with an *Acer palmatum* "Atropurpureum". If kept in check with surplus growth cut back it will make an excellent edging plant around a large circular container planted with liliums. All ajuga varieties make good subjects for hanging baskets, combined with annuals such as lobelia and petunias, or with ivies and pelargoniums. Be sure to water ajuga regularly as the plant should not be allowed to dry out.

Alternanthera *(Alternanthera bettzickiana).* This low-growing plant is normally used in the garden as a groundcover or edging plant, and will very soon fill a hanging basket to overflowing if planted on its own, showing off its red, pink or yellow foliage. It can also be used to underplant palms, ficus and syzygium in containers. Alternanthera is tender to frost and needs warm conditions.

A healthy aspidistra has been given a "skirt" of peace in the home.

Asparagus ferns *(Asparagus plumosus)* are useful for their attractive, feathery, green foliage, and are particularly good for baskets or containers. *A. sprengeri*, also an evergreen perennial, has fine, pointed leaves which makes it ideal for trailing over the edge of a container. Asparagus ferns need plenty of space to come to their best, but if the container is big enough they will look attractive planted around a central palm tree, or planted in the centre of a container with vinca trailing over the edge. Asparagus ferns are frost tender

A phormium planted in a fairly tall pot to show its shape to good advantage. Chlorophytums in troughs have a similar leaf shape to complete the picture.

and need a sheltered, semi-shaded position. They will take well to being planted with impatiens.

Aspidistra *(Aspidistra elatior)*, an evergreen perennial with clusters of attractive, shiny leaves is, sadly, often overlooked by gardeners. It is aptly called the cast-iron plant for its ability to withstand adverse conditions and will grow in shady, dark corners where few other plants may survive. Plant it in a pretty pot on the patio, or in a large container under the trees.

Begonias *(Begonia spp.)*. Several begonias are valued for their leaves, including the rex begonia *(B. rex)* and the iron cross begonia *(B. masoniana)*. They relish semi-shade, rich, loose soil and plenty of water from spring through summer. They are tender to frost and should be grown in a sheltered part of the patio, or place their container in the garden during summer and bring them indoors when the cold weather comes. Maidenhair ferns and myosotis will make excellent company. Tree begonias, or cane begonias *(B. coccinea)* have long, slender canes bearing well-shaped leaves and heads of pink or white flowers. Impatiens, ferns and ivies will add to their cool look. The leafy begonias are also beautiful on their own to show off their splendid leaves.

Caladiums *(Caladium bicolor)* are tuberous perennials and come in a great variety of colour combinations. Those with predominantly pink leaves will blend well with a cordyline with pink or maroon leaves, or with dieffenbachias, aglaonemas and ferns for a luxuriant, truly tropical combination. They do not like frost, but can be brought to the patio to display their magnificent colours when in full leaf in summer, and moved to a sheltered place when the cold weather comes. Plant them in compost-rich soil.

Callisia *(Callisia repens)* has a dense growth of small, round leaves which are green on the upper surface, and purple on the underside. It quickly forms neat cushions of growth, and while it makes a good specimen plant, it is also valued for its ability to form a groundcover between taller plants, among them crotons and acalyphas. Callisia will also look attractive planted among tree ferns and palms.

Coleus *(Coleus blumei)*. This annual of brightly coloured leaves in reds, purples, yellows and greens thrives in shade or semi-shade and grows well in containers, but needs protection from the wind. Pinch out the flowers as they appear, and take cuttings to keep up the supply. Coleus makes a statement on its own, but will also combine readily with impatiens, pansies and violas. Mix them with petunias and lobelias in hanging baskets, and use them to underplant a fuchsia standard.

In a sub-tropical garden an attractive grouping of leafy subjects of diverse shapes and many shades of green is drawn together by the clay jar with an aged look.

CREEPING JENNY *(Lysimachia nummularia)*, a quick-growing, ever-green perennial, is normally used in the garden as a groundcover. With its clear, gold leaves and yellow flowers, it will be a wonderful foil for blue lobelias or deep purple pansies if planted on the outer edge of a windowbox or container so that it can tumble over the side. It does well in a shady position.

CTENANTHE *(Ctenanthe lubbersiana)*, with its long oval leaves of green, blotched in pale yellow, favours a warm climate, and must have shelter in cold climates. *C. oppenheimiana* "Tricolor" has colourful leaves streaked in white, grey and green with burgundy undersides, bringing a luxuriant look wherever it is planted. Plant it in well-drained soil in shade or semi-shade, together with ferns, callisia or caladiums, and keep it moist.

DIEFFENBACHIAS *(Dieffenbachia spp.)* are very popular as indoor plants, but they will also do well in a shady, sheltered position on the patio, or, in a warm garden, they will look handsome in large pots. They like good, strong light, but not direct sunlight and their handsome leaves will be damaged by wind. Plant a group of dieffenbachias in fairly shallow containers in the shade of tree ferns. Regular feeding with liquid manure will ensure that the leaves maintain their attractive colours.

DRACAENAS *(Dracaena spp.)* bear their leaves in whorls around a central stem, and may range in colour from the plain dark green of the indigenous species, to *D. marginata* "Tricolor", with leaves striped in cream and green, margined with pink. They are frost tender and very much part of the sub-tropical garden where, grown in containers in shade or semi-shade, they will lend height to surrounding containers planted with ferns, caladiums and other foliage plants. They need lots of water and good drainage.

FURCRAEA *(Furcraea foetida)* is a spectacular foliage plant with long, sword-shaped leaves. The leaves of *F. foetida* "Striata" are striped in green and cream, arranged in a rosette, resembling an agave. Plant it in a container surrounded with pebbles or gravel and place it where it will not detract from other plants.

HELICHRYSUM *(Helichrysum petiolare)* sends out long, slender stems bearing round, grey leaves. It likes full sun and is tolerant of poor soil. It is highly useful for windowboxes where it will cascade over the edge, and mixes well with pelargoniums, vincas and pink or purple petunias.

HEN AND CHICKENS *(Chlorophytum comosum)*. This indigenous plant with its long, green or variegated leaves, and its habit of sending out long stems, makes it a good plant for windowboxes and hanging baskets. It prefers semi-shade and needs plenty of water. Plant a windowbox or large hanging basket with bright red impatiens and allow chlorophytum to cascade over the edge, or use them to underplant a standard ficus.

HOSTAS *(Hosta sieboldiana)* are becoming more readily available, and are worth having for their good-looking leaves of green, or variegated in cream or gold. They are greedy feeders and do best in the shade. Hostas will mix well with ferns and impatiens if they are placed in large containers where they can be left for several years.

HOUTTUYNIA *(Houttuynia cordata* "Chamaeleon") is often planted near water, but also makes a good groundcover with its leaves variegated in pink, green and cream. Preferring shade or semi-shade, it can be planted in a container with tree ferns, impatiens or fuchsias, and cascading over the edge of a basket, it will be a suitable companion for tall liliums.

HYPOESTES *(Hypoestes phyllostachya* "Freckle Face") has pink spots on its green leaves, and with its low-growing habit makes a charming accompaniment for cordylines, dracaenas, acalyphas and crotons. It is tender to frost and must be kept moist.

KALE *(Brassica oleracea* var. *acephala)*. Ornamental or curly kale is grown mainly as a decorative plant but is also used as a garnishing in salads. It looks like a painted cabbage with its curly, variegated green, red, white or purple leaves. Looking its best in winter, it makes a talking point wherever it is shown. Plant individual plants in separate pots, then bring them together in ornamental containers.

LIRIOPE *(Liriope muscari)* is a perennial with grass-like leaves of green, gold or variegations, and sends up slender stems of lilac-coloured, bell-like flowers. It looks attractive all year round as an edging plant and is frost hardy which makes it a very useful plant for cold gardens.

MOSAIC PLANT *(Fittonia verschaffeltii* "Argyroneura") is an ornamental, evergreen perennial with particularly decorative foliage of ovate green leaves with prominent white veins. Use it to underplant shade lovers, and give it a warm, humid position away from draughts.

PEACOCK PLANT *(Calathea makoyana)* is one of the many foliage plants that thrive in hot, humid conditions, bearing large leaves with many markings and variations. Grown in the shade, in rich, friable soil with plenty of water, it will go well with caladiums, ferns or ajuga.

PHORMIUMS *(Phormium spp.)* thrive in a sunny position and have been hybridized into many new colours and sizes. *P. cookianum* "Tricolor" has leaves striped in yellow and green, and *P. tenax* "Bronze Baby" has upright-growing, burgundy leaves. There are many other varieties of this versatile family suitable for container planting. Particularly suitable as accent plants, they also mix well with other plants. Place a "Bronze Baby" in a flat, round container surrounded with crimson tulips, or place a "Tricolor" in an Aladdin jar on either side of a flight of steps.

PRAYER PLANT *(Maranta leuconeura)*. Also known as ten commandments, *M. leuconeura* "Erythroneura" has oval leaves with a cream mid-rib and veins heavily marked in scarlet. As it has a habit of lying close to the ground, it is ideal for planting in a large container where it can act as a groundcover under tall tree ferns and blechnums. It does best in moist sub-tropical conditions and must have well-drained soil.

SENECIO *(Senecio maritima)* has finely divided leaves of silver-grey. It will blend well with pink petunias in a hanging basket, or tone down bright purple pansies. Try planting it with both pink and purple petunias. Plant a windowbox with pink ivy-leafed pelargoniums, vivid scarlet zonal pelargoniums or lavenders and allow senecio and *Helichrysum petiolare* to cascade from the edge. Purple or pink verbenas will also mix well with their grey leaves. Their small yellow flowers should be removed before they mature to keep up a good leaf growth.

TRADESCANTIAS *(Tradescantia spp.)* can act as groundcovers or trailing plants and are valued for pots and baskets. *T. fluminensis* (wandering Jew) is striped in green and cream, making it a good foil for dark green ferns, or for the vividly coloured "New Guinea" hybrid impatiens. *T. pallida* "Purple Heart" has deep purple leaves which will contrast beautifully with ivy-leafed pelargoniums. They are frost tender and need a sunny position. As they spread rather quickly they may need regular cutting back.

VINCA *(Vinca major)* with plain green leaves, and *V. major* "Variegata" both have a trailing habit, their tender stems bearing small oval leaves. Their trailing habit makes them useful for baskets where they will mix with ivies, lobelias, pelargoniums and petunias. They do well in both sun and shade.

Hostas are prone to attack by insects, including grasshoppers, and preventive measures should be taken in early spring.

Right: "Temple Fire" bougainvillea. Opposite: The straight lines of a standard set in a square container are off-set by the rounded form of the empty jar.

CHAPTER 6

Trees, Shrubs and Climbers in Containers

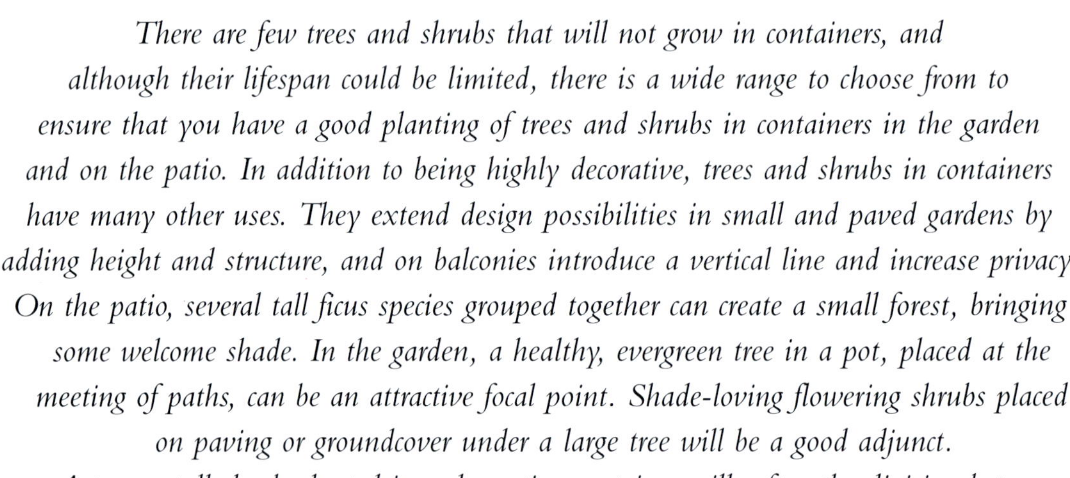

There are few trees and shrubs that will not grow in containers, and although their lifespan could be limited, there is a wide range to choose from to ensure that you have a good planting of trees and shrubs in containers in the garden and on the patio. In addition to being highly decorative, trees and shrubs in containers have many other uses. They extend design possibilities in small and paved gardens by adding height and structure, and on balconies introduce a vertical line and increase privacy. On the patio, several tall ficus species grouped together can create a small forest, bringing some welcome shade. In the garden, a healthy, evergreen tree in a pot, placed at the meeting of paths, can be an attractive focal point. Shade-loving flowering shrubs placed on paving or groundcover under a large tree will be a good adjunct.

A tree or tall shrub planted in a decorative container will soften the division between two garages, while several container-grown trees will soften the paving around the pool without the danger of roots lifting the paving. Trees and shrubs in containers add interest to steps or entrances. They will also make a statement, defining the entrance to another section of the garden. A tree or shrub in a pot, underplanted with trailing ivy, will not only camouflage an unsightly manhole, but become an attractive feature in the garden without restricting access to the manhole.

Above: The conical wooden structure placed in the container will soon be covered by the trachelospermum creeper which bears a mass of fragrant white flowers.

Advantages of Containers

The biggest advantage of growing trees and shrubs in containers, is that there is no need to interfere with patio paving for planting. Another good reason for planting trees and shrubs in containers is that many of them have vigorous root systems which, on the patio, or even in the garden, could cause chaos. Most ficus species are notorious for this crime. Plant them in the garden

and in no time at all their roots will have spread far and wide, causing walls to collapse, and paths to rise, and yet they have a great attraction in containers. Other trees, such as liquidambars, could grow far too large for the small garden, yet in a large container they may be beautiful, bringing their quota of autumn glory, and full foliage in summer. The same applies to several indigenous trees such as *Celtis africana* (white stinkwood) and *Halleria lucida* (tree fuchsia).

Container-grown trees and shrubs can also be moved around with the changing weather, enabling you to grow frost-tender plants which may not survive in the open garden. Acid lovers such as camellias, azaleas and pieris, would probably not do well in heavily alkaline soil, but if you plant them in containers, you can control their environment by using acid soil and compost in the pot.

Pure white tulips and primulas bring a light-hearted air to the rather formal trees planted in a variety of containers.

Choice of Containers

Containers should be strong, durable and big enough. Any tree or shrub which is going to grow to a fairly large size will need to sit comfortably in its container, so don't stint on the size. A half wine barrel will allow a tree to grow to a height of at least 2 m. Wooden tubs are of a good size, and there are many fibre-cement, terracotta and concrete pots which will easily house large trees and shrubs (*also see* p. 20). Most trees and large shrubs will last for several years in a pot with a depth of 75 cm, if it is filled with a good soil mix, before repotting is necessary.

Generally, tall plants are better in tall containers – a tall conifer would not look right in a flat dish. However, palms, with their surface roots, will grow well in fairly flat containers. A very pleasant effect can be achieved by planting a tree such as an acer (maple) into a large, relatively flat pot, and underplanting it with groundcovers, bulbs or cascading annuals – a self-contained garden.

Planting and Routine Care

Specific growing conditions will naturally vary with the plants, depending on their natural habitat, but a good general soil for trees and shrubs in containers can be made up of three parts good garden soil, one half well-rotted manure, one half compost and one part coarse sand and a sprinkling of bone meal.

Add a generous handful of superphosphates and a slow-release fertilizer for every 10 litres of soil and mix well. There are also good commercial mixes available, which have been carefully formulated.

When planting a new tree or shrub, examine the roots and cleanly cut away any damaged parts. Plant it at the same level as in the bag in which it was bought and stake it, if necessary, to keep it upright. Water, and lightly firm the soil. The soil should be about 2,5 cm from the top of the container. Check on the soil level and adjust if necessary.

Bear in mind that the roots of plants in containers standing in the sun become extremely hot, so watering, especially in hot weather, is of vital importance. This, in turn, calls for extreme-

QUICK TOPIARY

A quick way of creating a topiary effect, is to make a wire or chicken-mesh frame, pack it closely with moss or hessian, and train a small-leafed ivy around the frame. Some nurseries sell readymade frames for this purpose. Suitable ivies for topiary will be those with small leaves, such as *Hedera helix* "Goldheart", "Glacier", "Little Diamond" and "Luzii".

Regular clipping of the side stems of ivies used for topiary will result in a full, neat and compact growth.

ly good drainage. A good layer of permanent mulch will ensure that the roots are kept cool.

As container plants are always on display, they must be kept in good appearance by constantly taking out any dead or straggly growth and clipping back unwanted growth. To ensure bushy growth, many shrubs and trees should have their terminal buds nipped back once or twice – this applies especially to evergreens such as syzygiums and murrayas.

Trees and shrubs with vigorous root systems can be kept in good health by trimming the roots and replenishing the soil (*see* p. 122). You can remove deciduous trees completely when they are dormant, trim their roots, then plant them back into their containers which have been replenished. Containers restrict root development and slow down the rate of growth, and if trees and shrubs become pot-bound they must be repotted (*see* p. 121).

Some trees and shrubs are more vigorous than others, so it is difficult to lay down rules for feeding, but generally, they can be given a dressing of general fertilizer in early spring, and another in late summer.

Conifers usually do not take kindly to chemical fertilizer, and should be given a good dose of liquid sea manure twice during the growing season, and kept well watered.

Some trees may need support to keep them upright, or, in the case of climbers, to encourage upward growth. A wigwam of sticks or thin planks is one answer. A central, sturdy stick may also suffice, but this should be buried well into the soil. Climbers will need support to help them to reach the pillar or pergola over which they will eventually climb.

A tall tree with massive foliage in a tall pot could easily be blown over by the wind, so it is best to place it in a sheltered position or alternatively, drive a sturdy stake all the way through the container soil and through one of the drainage holes, to anchor it. If by doing this you limit the drainage, it will be necessary to make an extra hole.

TOPIARY

Pruning or training trees and shrubs into artificial shapes has come back into fashion, and is highly suited to

A syzygium's dark, evergreen leaves have been severely clipped to create an almost spherical shape, with an edging of alter-

container-grown plants. Choose small-leafed plants with dense growth, such as syzygium, buxus, conifers and euonymus, and start pruning them when they are young. Once started, it must be kept up. In the early stages, the outer growth can be kept clipped back, but with growth, you may need a stick or plank to keep to the straight lines of a cone, for instance. Alternatively, make a template of the required shape, place it over the plant and prune around it.

Choosing the Plants

While almost any tree or shrub will grow in a container, some are better suited to container planting than others, and special care should be taken when you choose your plants. There are several factors to be taken into account.

Do you want a deciduous or an evergreen tree? Evergreens look more or less the same all year through, but deciduous trees have tender green leaves in spring, and in autumn, bring a bounty of brilliant colours. Evergreens will need attention throughout the year, while deciduous plants become dormant, and need the minimum of attention during winter. Many evergreen trees and shrubs have lovely flowers, and others variegated leaves to break the monotony of green (*see* plant discussion).

What shape do you want – tall and slender, short and fat, spreading far and wide? Shapes vary enormously, and they can change the look of their surroundings greatly – tall and slender conifers will be elegant, whereas cordylines have a Mediterranean look; bamboos, on the other hand, are oriental, and trees and shrubs with a round growth-form, such as coprosmas and euonymus, can be charmingly informal.

Are the containers to be placed in the shade or sun? Some trees and shrubs can put up with a great deal of sun during the day, and others prefer shady conditions, some will grow in either. Some shade lovers will grow in the sun as long as they are kept mulched and watered. (*See* plant discussion.)

Many plants which are frost-tender can be grown in containers, to be put on display during the warm months in the garden or patio, then placed in a sheltered place during cold spells.

Opposite: The top growth of the standard azaleas is regularly clipped during summer.

Left: Dwarf nandina's close growth takes on rich autumnal colours.

Below: Ornamental kale makes an unusual and effective groundcover for standards.

• Trees, Shrubs and Climbers for Containers •

ABELIA *(Abelia floribunda)* makes an excellent ornamental shrub and can be kept in good shape by constant clipping. The variegated, golden-leafed "Francis Mason" is particularly attractive, bearing white, bell-shaped flowers in summer, while its bright foliage will highlight its place in any sunny spot in the garden. Underplant it with lysimachia (creeping Jenny) for an all gold look, or with *Ajuga reptans* or seasonal annuals such as phlox.

for standards.
Above: Double lollipops look striking in lattice containers
Opposite: A superb glazed ceramic container of royal blue, set against a coprosma, makes a striking cameo. Next to it alami-

ACALYPHAS *(Acalypha spp.)* are tropical plants and do not like frost, but in warmer areas, these evergreen shrubs put on a splendid display. Especially valued for their foliage, full sun brings out their colours, ranging from crimson and pink to green and white. They will also grow in semi-shade. They need plenty of water at all times. Acalyphas will spread their lower branches to fill a large container, and can be grouped with cordylines and dracaenas of similar colours.

AGAVES (*Agave spp.*). *A. americana* has long, wide fleshy leaves of green and cream stripes, ending with a sharp spine. It is best planted in a container on its own as an accent plant. *A. attenuata* has grey-green leaves in a neat rosette. Plant it in a circular, rather shallow container, surrounded with ajuga or lysimachia as groundcover, both of which are low growing and will not detract from the shape of the agave.

ALLAMANDA *(Allamanda cathartica)* is a sub-tropical, evergreen, rambling climber which will cascade over its container, or can be given a frame for support. In summer it bears clear gold, trumpet-shaped flowers, beautifully offset against its shiny, dark green leaves. This frost-tender plant needs a sunny position and frequent watering. Combine it with blue torenias in summer, and yellow and blue pansies or violas in spring.

ARTEMISIA *(Artemisia spp.).* These small, hardy, evergreen shrubs are known for their delicate silvery-grey foliage which makes them excellent contrast plants.. They need full sun and well-drained soil. Their grey foliage is a lovely foil for pink and purple petunias and purple lobelias. Surround it with purple and yellow pansies in a round container for a charming picture.

AZALEAS *(Rhododendron spp.)* look splendid in containers in a sheltered, semi-shaded position. The most popular azaleas locally are the evergreen "Kurume", "Indica" and "Wonder" hybrids with dark green leaves and single or double flowers in many colours. Deciduous azaleas (including "Mollis" and hybrids such as "Springvale" and "Exbury") have magnificent flowers, but are only suitable for cool, moist areas. Azaleas must have acid, well-drained soil. Use one of the special mixes, or add a tablespoon of ammonium sulphate for every 10 litres of soil. Their surface roots will need a constant mulch of pine needles or oak leaves.

BAMBOOS (various genera) are tall and slender with attractive stems, such as *Bambusa ventricosa* which is excellent for tubs, or low growing, such as *Phyllostachys multiplex* which forms a compact bush. They can be combined in a large container. Golden bamboo *(P.*

aurea) makes an attractive accent plant. *Pleioblastus auricoma* is a low-growing ornamental dwarf bamboo with leaves variegated in green and white. It works well for underplanting taller bamboos. Place the containers in a warm, sheltered position and keep the plants moist.

Bay tree *(Laurus nobilis)*. This evergreen tree is normally used as a focal point in a herb garden, but the shining green leaves make it an asset in any sunny position. Remove its lower leaves and underplant it with thyme, lemon balm and parsley.

Bougainvilleas *(Bougainvillea x cultivars)* are colourful, evergreen climbers which make good subjects for outdoor containers. Some varieties such as "Temple Fire" and "Bijou" are particularly suited to container planting and can be trained to climb over a pergola, but will need support. They need good drainage and full sun. Take special care when you plant bougainvilleas as they are notorious for taking badly to transplanting. Prepare the container as for other trees and shrubs, half fill with soil, then place the entire bag in which you bought the plant into the container at the right level. Make vertical slits around the bag to allow the roots to grow through, fill the container with soil, and water in the normal way to allow the soil to settle, and adjust the soil level, if necessary. Water the new plant regularly until it is established. After its first flowering period, cut it back, feed and water, then, as soon as a good set of foliage has developed, cut back on water and food to encourage further flowering. This cycle should be continued throughout.

Box *(Buxus spp.)*. This evergreen, rounded shrub with its fine, dense leaves, can be clipped and shaped beautifully, and lends itself to topiary. Although slow growing, it grows well in all parts of the country in sun or semi-shade, and is frost hardy.

Camellias *(Camellia spp.)*. These evergreen trees and shrubs are lovely container subjects for balconies, patios or verandahs. *C. sasanqua* does well in the sun, and in the shade is a valuable foliage plant. It must have a container with good width to allow its feeding roots to spread, and a constant mulch. Camellias need plenty of water. If grown in containers in the garden, they can be kept to a good shape, and used in groups, or placed on either side of a statue, they impart a classic look.

Calamondin *(Citrus mitis)*. This miniature citrus is a charming plant for containers, looking most attractive in a wooden barrel on the patio. It is usually trained into a round shape, bearing a multitude of small, edible oranges in winter, and looks attractive underplanted with flowering annuals or herbs. Plant calamondin in moderately heavy soil with a good amount of well-rotted kraal manure and compost – up to a third of the bulk. During the growing season, starting in spring, give calamondin trees a generous sprinkling of general fertilizer followed by a good soaking immediately afterwards, with regular, deep watering. The tree should never be allowed to dry out completely.

Carissa *(Carissa macrocarpa)*. Also known as the Natal Plum, carissa is an indigenous, evergreen shrub with a close growth of shining leaves. White, star-shaped flowers in early summer are followed by edible red fruit. The "Green Carpet" variety has a cascading growth. It does best in full sun and although it is semi-hardy, it will not tolerate heavy frost.

Clematis *(Clematis spp.)*, one of the loveliest of deciduous climbing plants, likes its feet in the shade and head in the sun. *C. montana* with its fragrant, white flowers, is more vigorous than the hybrids, and is best left on its own in a container, whereas the hybrids, which bloom from late spring to early summer, will look lovely with cascading petunias or spring bulbs such as Dutch irises, or groundcover roses such as "Flower Carpet" or "Pink Sunsation". Clematis needs plenty of extra food during summer when growth is vigorous. The hybrids must be cut back hard after the flowering period in late summer and autumn (the cuttings can be planted). They will die down to come into new growth in spring. Clematis looks good planted near a dainty rather than a heavy frame.

Conifers – *see* Special Container Plants p. 83.

Above: Camellias will do well in pots if regularly fed and watered, the water thoroughly saturating the well-drained soil.
Left: Autumn brings out the vibrant colours of the nandinas, as well as the fruits of calamondin.
Opposite: Double bougainvillea "Princess Maharani".

Coprosmas *(Coprosma repens)* with their spreading, cascading habit, usually fill their pot, leaving little space for other plants, with the exception of *C. kirkii* "Variegata" which has a slender growth and will go well with dwarf conifers, *Felicia amelloides*, and *Convolvulus sabatius* (ground morning glory). Their generous, colourful foliage of green and various variegations such as pink and coffee-coloured, will act as a fine foil for other container plants placed below them, such as dark green ivy, variegated vinca, *Begonia semperflorens* or the trailing *Gazania rigens uniflora*. This hardy, evergreen shrub is very adaptable but prefers a sunny position, especially for the variegated varieties, such as "Picturata" with its large leaves with golden-yellow centres.

Coral berry *(Ardisia crenulata)*. This small, slow-growing shrub is shaped like a tree, with shining leaves and scarlet berries providing splashes of colour in winter. Plant several together in a container, underplanted with moss, and place in a shady, sheltered position on the patio as they are tender to frost.

Cordylines *(Cordyline spp.)*. Some of these evergreen, palm-like trees have highly decorative leaves, some have plain green leaves, borne in whorls around a slender central stem. *C. australis*, with leaves of either green or bronze, is hardy and can grow very tall. It is an excellent specimen plant and will look particularly attractive as the centrepiece of a grouping. Surround it with *Nandina domestica* "Pygmaea", or, more striking, give it a carpet of tulips in season. *C. terminalis* hybrids grow well in sub-tropical, frost-free areas where they are an asset in semi-shaded parts. They will look attractive when underplanted with trailing groundcovers or ferns. Many cordylines have leaves in shades of burgundy and pink, and go well with caladiums of similar shading, or with pink alternanthera or *Soleirolia soleirolii* (peace in the home). Cordylines prefer fertile, well-drained soil. They do best in full sun or semi-shade and must be watered regularly.

A striking contrast of scarlet tulips and a burgundy cordyline. Left: The different shapes and textures of the containers are shown to perfection against the dark green virginia creeper.

Crotons *(Codiaeum variegatum)* have highly coloured leaves in shades of pink and burgundy, gold, pale yellow, various shades of green and many variegations. They thrive in full sun or semi-shade in the hot, humid, sub-tropical regions. These evergreen shrubs make good container plants, growing to a large size. Plant them with caladiums, chlorophytums and cordylines. In cooler regions, they can be grown on the patio, until the cold weather arrives, when they should be moved to a warm, sheltered position with lots of light.

Elaeagnus *(Elaeagnus pungens)* is a hardy, evergreen shrub with oval, leathery leaves. Although slow growing, it will tolerate poor weather conditions. Especially valued for their foliage, the variegated varieties with combinations of green and white, green and yellow, and yellow, pink and white leaves are the most popular. Place containers in a sunny position for the best show of colours.

Euonymus *(Euonymus spp.)* has come into its own of late, with many new varieties. *E. japonicus* has plain green leaves, but there are many hybrids, with variegations of green and gold, which are smaller and make ideal container plants. They are good topiary plants that can be clipped to round or columnar shape, or they can be trained into standards, underplanted with variegated vinca, nasturtiums, mauve allysum, and ajuga, or in warmer regions, alternanthera. *E. fortunei* "Emerald Gaiety" has emerald green leaves margined in silver, and with its creeping habit makes an ideal plant for hanging baskets, or for planting under taller euonymus. Try mixing it with vivid blue lobelias and *Begonia semperflorens.* These attractive, evergreen shrubs are hardy and adaptable to different climates.

This classically shaped, decorated urn, with its planting of a standard, ivy and begonias, will be an elegant addition to any uninteresting corner.

Ferns – *see* Special Container Plants p. 92.

Ficus *(Ficus spp.).* The fig genus has given us many very useful evergreen varieties, including self-clinging climbers, suitable for containers. *F. benjamina* (weeping fig) has been given twisted stems, but is as attractive in its natural shape and will last for many years in a container, growing well in spite of its confined conditions, as will *F. elastica* (rubber tree), some varieties of which have variegated leaves. *F hawaii* is slender with variegated leaves, and *F. pumila,* the popular tickey creeper, can be grown like ivy up trellis and pillars. Place their containers in a sunny, sheltered position as most ficus species are frost tender. Slender ficus trees can be underplanted with a large variety of plants: annuals such as begonias, petunias, lobelias and alyssum will do well, as will ornamental kale and many species of groundcovers, including ajuga, lamium and vinca. Or plant several *Chlorophytum comosum* (hen and chickens) around the edge to cascade over the container.

Frangipani *(Plumeria spp.)* is most suitable for warm, moist regions, but will grow in most frost-free areas. It could be a talking point on the patio, where it will delight with its fragrant yellow or pink flowers. Keeping a frangipani in a container will restrict its growth, but it can be kept in check by cutting back the branches, which will give rise to a more compact growth. Care should be taken with the milky sap which may burn the eyes or skin. Use ordinary soil in the container and do not give too much food or water.

Fuchsias – *see* Special Container Plants p. 87.

Heavenly bamboo *(Nandina domestica).* This evergreen shrub comes in two forms. The tall species with its straight, slender stems grows up to two metres and more, which is ideal for creating a woodland effect, or for placing at the edge of a water feature. As it has a habit of spreading by suckers, it is better if confined to a container. *N. domestica* "Pygmaea" is, as its name implies, a dwarf type, forming compact mounds of leaves which change to rich crimson and gold in autumn. It can be used to underplant the taller variety, *Cordyline australis* or "Skyrocket" conifers. Place in a sunny, wind-sheltered position and water frequently during hot spells.

Hibiscus *(Hibiscus rosa-sinensis)* have a wonderful exotic look, with their large, satiny flowers and shiny, green leaves. Evergreen and quick growing, they make good standards, and good container plants. Generally they do best in full sun. *H. rosa-sinensis* "Natensis" has variegated leaves of green and white

Containers add their quota of green to the lush surroundings. Left: Happy cats and a friendly bird stand guard over a beautiful bonsai fig tree on a sheltered patio.

and *H. rosa-sinensis* "Cooperi" is variegated in pink, red and white and will grow in shade or semi-shade. Regular feeding and watering are essential in the growing season from spring through to autumn.

Holly *(Ilex spp.)* has attractive, spiny leaves and bright red berries. Some varieties of the evergreen species have variegated leaves. English holly *(I. aquifolium)* does best in cool, moist regions, while Chinese holly *(I. cornuta)*, which bears its berries in winter, is more suited to warmer areas. Prune regularly to keep them in shape. Because of their prickly leaves it is difficult to find companions for hollies, but as they are evergreen, they have year-round interest. A groundcover of ivy under a potted holly will make a lovely combination for Christmas. An underplanting of *Liriope muscari* "Variegata" with its gold-edged leaves could also be a good foil, as could *Lamium galeobdolon.*

Honeysuckle *(Lonerica spp.)* can be used as a climber, or as a self-standing shrub by judicious clipping, and giving it suitable support. Clusters of fragrant pink, red or white and yellow flowers appear in spring or summer. These shrubs are hardy and will grow in full sun or semi-shade. Dwarf white or blue agapanthus with their upright stems will be a fine contrast for the free growth of lonerica. If lonerica is grown up a frame, there should be space in the container for one or two *Lilium longiflora*, or for the rose "Sweet Chariot", or even both. For an old-fashioned look, plant lavender in front of lonericas.

Hoya *(Hoya carnosa)*, the wax plant, is a most obliging evergreen climber and a popular container plant. It will grow from a relatively small container, sending up its long stems to bear clusters of waxy, fragrant blooms. Although it will grow up a pergola or a frame, its growth is not heavy and prolific. Hoyas only grow in areas which have no frost. Where light frost occurs, they can be grown in a sheltered, sunny part of the patio. They need a well-drained mixture of sand, loam and compost, and regular watering and feeding to encourage a good growth of leaves. Cut down on food and water once there is a good growth of foliage to encourage buds and flowers to form. Resume nourishment after the flowering period. *H. bella*, with its compact growth, is an excellent subject for a hanging basket. *H. carnosa*'s lower growth is sparse, and a covering of echeverias or other succulents will not only look attractive, but the succulents will withstand the almost drought-like conditions required for good blooming of the hoya.

Hydrangeas – *see* Special Container Plants p. 94.

Ivy *(Hedera spp.)*. One of the best-loved, evergreen climbing plants, ivy is hardy and easy to grow. There are many varieties, of green and variegation. *H. helix* "Goldheart" has a tiny, golden heart in its green leaves, "Glacier" has white edges around its glossy green leaves, "Buttercup" has leaves of pale gold and "Gloire de Marengo" has deep green leaves edged in cream. Most ivies thrive in full sun or semi-shade and are frost tolerant. They can be used as a groundcover under taller trees and shrubs, and can even be encouraged to climb up into its host. In windowboxes and hanging baskets they mix well with other cascading plants such as lobelias, *Helichrysum petiolare* or ivy-leafed pelargoniums. Ivy can also be used to climb over wire-mesh shapes to resemble topiary (*see* p. 65). Plant ivy on its own in a container, with an urn or bust placed in the centre, and allow it to fill the container to overflowing.

A demure maiden among the ivy leaves in a wide, shallow pot placed on a low pedestal to allow the ivy to cascade freely.

Kumquats *(Fortunella japonica)* are grown successfully in containers. Their tiny, orange-like fruits, borne from early spring to mid-autumn, are not only highly decorative, but also edible and are often used in preserves. It needs well-drained, organically rich soil. Regular, light pruning and pinching out the tips of the stems will ensure a small, compact tree which looks attractive underplanted with chlorophytum, lysimachia and "Buttercup" ivy.

Liquidambars *(Liquidambar styraciflua)* are among the most colourful deciduous trees in autumn, their finger-like leaves turning to crimson, purple and yellow. It will grow well in a wide container filled with well-drained soil. It should not be overfed or overwatered which will make for overly vigorous growth, but should also not be allowed to dry out during the spring and summer months. It may be necessary to trim the roots after three of four years (*see* p. 122). Spring bulbs, such as freesias, sparaxis and muscari planted under the tree, will bloom when it is bare of leaves, and in summer impatiens will bloom in its shade. For a more permanent underplanting, use mondo grass *(Ophiopogon japonicus)* or liriope.

Mandevilla *(Mandevilla splendens)*. This popular, evergreen climber will grow in a container on the patio, trained up a frame or pergola, but it must have a good circulation of air around it. Tender to wind and frost, it needs a sunny, sheltered position, for which it will reward you with splendid pink flowers from early summer well into autumn.

Maples *(Acer spp.)*. Most maples grow well in containers. Being deciduous, they change colour in autumn, then become dormant, when you can cut down on watering. They can be trimmed into a good shape by removing any twiggy growth and by taking off the lower branches to allow for underplanting with other plants. Acers like to be kept damp, with a cool root run and a permanent mulch. Particularly attractive for container planting are the smaller varieties with variegated leaves. The weeping Japanese maple *(A. palmatum)* will grow in a fairly shallow container as long as it is kept damp, which makes it highly suitable for placing it where it can overhang a water feature. Upright maples look lovely underplanted with alyssum or white *Primula malacoides*, with pots of white tulips placed next to them. For a more colourful display, plant any winter and spring bulbs which will bloom under the bare branches.

Melaleuca *(Melaleuca bracteata* "Johannesburg gold") with its feathery leaves of gold, makes a fine background for lower-growing plants. It needs a good sized container to accommodate its roots. This hardy, evergreen shrub is ideal for coastal gardens, as well as those in cooler areas, and grows well in full sun.

A demure maiden among the ivy leaves in a wide, shallow pot placed on a low pedestal to allow the ivy to cascade freely. Above: Acers in various containers create a miniature forest.

Orange jessamine *(Murraya exotica)* has dark green leaves, and bears fragrant white flowers in spring and summer. It is ideal for topiary work. Trained into a standard it can be given a carpet of white alyssum, white *Begonia semperflorens*, or blue lobelias. Place

its container in a sunny, wind-sheltered position and protect the plant from frost.

Palms – *see* Special Container Plants p. 99.

Philodendrons *(Philodendron spp.).* These handsome, evergreen, robust climbers and shrubs with their attractive green foliage will thrive in a surprisingly small container, as long as the leaves are regularly sprayed with a mister. *P. scandens* has heart-shaped leaves and will need plenty of space in a corner of the patio. Old growth must be constantly cut right back to the main stem to encourage vigorous new growth. *P. selloum* has heavily indented leaves while "Emerald Queen" is particularly attractive as its leaves have an attractive burgundy colour on the underside. Grown in containers outdoors, philodendrons need a warm, moist shady position. As they are such striking plants, they are best left on their own in a sheltered corner of the patio or garden.

Polyscias *(Polyscias filicifolia)* with their feathery, fern-like golden leaves come to their best in full sun, but, as they may be burnt by high winds, need a sheltered position in the garden or on the patio. They grow into slender shrubs which resemble small trees. Plant several in a wide container, underplanted with mondo grass or golden lamium, or bright blue ageratums, torenias, begonias or impatiens for seasonal colour. The green leaves of *P. scuttelaria* "Balfourii" are more like those of a maple. It thrives in warm, humid conditions and will grow in the shade in subtropical areas, accompanied by maidenhair ferns.

Privets *(Ligustrum spp.)* form a thick mat of invasive roots, so it is practical to treat them as container plants on their own, where they can reach into the sur-

rounding soil without depriving other plants of nourishment. The golden privet *(L. ovalifolium* "Aureamarginatum"), a fast-growing, evergreen shrub with bright yellow and green leaves, is particularly attractive and tolerates most weather conditions except severe frost. Privets do best in full sun or semi-shade. Place a container of golden privets among other containered foliage plants such as *Abelia floribunda* "Francis Mason", golden conifers such as "Goldcrest" or, for contrast, with *Phormium tenax* "Variegatum".

PYRACANTHAS *(Pyracantha spp.)* are dense, evergreen shrubs which bloom and bear berries at an early age, and so are worthwhile plants for containers. "Santa Cruz" and "Orange Charmer" are two hybrids which will take well to potting. Keep them clipped back when they are young to ensure bushy growth, or, if they are to be trained up a wigwam, start training the stems when they are young. Pyracanthas are hardy and prefer full sun.

ROSES – *see* Special Container Plants p. 103.

STAR JASMINE *(Trachelospermum jasminoides)* is an evergreen climber with dark green leaves and fragrant, white, star-shaped flowers in spring and summer. It needs a rich soil, and will grow over a frame placed in its container, or will tumble over an arch or pergola. It is frost hardy and grows well in full sun as long as the roots are shaded. Trachelospermum can be used in a windowbox as a trailing plant, but its growth is too vigorous for it to last long in a hanging basket. If planted in a container with a wigwam of slats, it will soon cover this with compact growth. It can also be planted close to the edge in a large container, tumbling over the sides, leaving space for a ficus in the centre. Keep it in check by constantly clipping back any old growth and nipping out new growth.

STRELITZIAS *(Strelitzia reginae)*. The striking crane flower will grow readily in a container sufficiently deep to take its fairly long roots. It grows in full sun and semi-shade, but is frost tender and needs a sheltered position. As it multiplies rapidly, plants must be divided every four or five years, taking the outer growth for replanting. As *S. reginae* is such a vigorous grower, it will not take kindly to having a companion in its pot. It will make a striking accent plant on any sunny patio or in a sunny paved area of the garden, and looks spectacular placed close to a *Petrea volubilis* or at the edge of a water feature.

STROBILANTHES *(Strobilanthes anisophyllus)* has decorative strap leaves of deep purple, making it a good plant for showing up the colour of other plants. A striking combination is that of strobilanthes underplanted with golden lysimachia (creeping Jenny). For a more gentle effect, give it a carpet of mauve *Primula malacoides* in spring. Chlorophytum will also be a striking contrast for this evergreen shrub which grows well in full sun or semi-shade, but is frost tender and needs a wind-sheltered position.

SYNGONIUM *(Syngonium podophyllum)*, also known as the goosefoot plant, is seen in many sub-tropical gardens where it acts as a groundcover under large trees and is valued as a climbing foliage plant. It will grow in a container up a frame or over a central column of sturdy cane, and will then overflow the container to create a charming, evergreen effect. Although it looks effective on its own, it can be used with palms such as *Howea fosteriana* or *Chrysalidocarpus lutescens*. Place it, with its container, on the patio where it can climb up a treillage, or out in a shady part of the garden, where it can be trained over a wooden framework. Syngonium needs warm, moist conditions.

SYZYGIUM *(Syzygium paniculatum)* is a lovely ornamental plant which will grow into a neat shrub in a container. It has attractive, evergreen, shining

Above: Beyond the circular brick container with aechmeas, is a fine selection of topiary trees and shrubs. Opposite: Syngonium "Silver Pearl" was given wire and moss for support.

leaves, and bears white feathery flowers followed by shocking pink fruit. It can be standardized by removing all side growth to the required height, then allowing the top growth to develop. It is ideal for topiary and if the top growth is pinched out in the early stages, it will create a compact bush which can be clipped into a ball shape or any other required shape. It is frost tender and needs a warm, sheltered position.

Tree fuchsia *(Halleria lucidia)* is an indigenous tree which bears its mass of flowers close to the stems. The flowers are filled with nectar, attracting many birds. Plant it in a large container filled with organically rich soil and water it regularly during summer. It can be trained into a standard, or, left alone, it will grow into a tree with dense foliage. Underplant it with *Plectranthus hilliardiae* or *P. madagascariensis* (spur flowers), clivias or indigenous ferns.

Umbrella tree *(Schefflera actinophylla)* is a handsome foliage plant, with glossy, fan-like leaves. It can grow quite tall, but if the growing tip is removed, it will branch out. *S. arboricola* "Variegata" has light yellow patches on its dark green leaves. It is frost tender and grows best in warm, moist areas. Place in a sheltered position in full sun or semi-shade, underplanted with *Plectranthus madagascariencis.*

White stinkwood *(Celtis africana)* will grow well in a container, provided that its roots are kept in check by regular pruning every two or three years in winter when it is dormant. Remove twiggy growth to keep it in good shape. Underplant the tree with dwarf agapanthus or ifafa lilies *(Cyrtanthus mackenii)* for a striking indigenous display.

Wisteria *(Wisteria sinensis).* This popular deciduous climber with its sprays of blue or white scented flowers need not take on a straggling and untidy appearance, but can be turned into an attractive standard for container planting. Keep one main stem and allow it to grow to the required height, then allow the top growth to develop blooms. After blooming, cut the top growth back to two or three buds on each of three or four stems, which are again allowed to develop. If this process is repeated every year, the wisteria in its container will become a focal point in the garden, or, if it is placed near a small water feature, will have a lovely weeping effect. Wisteria is a vigorous climber and makes a good cover for a pergola, providing shade in summer, while letting the sun shine through its bare branches in winter.

Yuccas *(Yucca filamentosa).* Striking, evergreen shrubs with sword-like leaves, often with spines at their ends, yuccas can be a danger where children are at play, and should be placed well out of their way. In mid-summer *Y. filamentosa* sends a single stem of creamy white flowers from its low rosette of leaves. *Y. gloriosa* has a short trunk and does not grow as tall as *Y. filamentosa.* Container-grown yuccas make excellent accent plants and need very little attention. Placed in a container at an entrance or at the head of a flight of steps, a yucca will have an instant impact. Give them a sunny position and well-drained soil.

A tapestry of mauve daisies enfolding a pot of echeverias. Opposite: An aged terracotta pot nestles amidst a wealth of sub-tropical foliage. Below: The simple, uncluttered lines of an "Iceberg" do not detract from a highly decorated container.

CHAPTER 7

Special Container Plants

Although every container plant is regarded as special by its owner, some plants are particularly popular, or especially suitable for container planting. This may be because these plants have a neat, compact growth habit, a longer flowering period, attractive foliage or a particularly interesting shape. Not everyone will necessarily agree that the selection in this chapter is representative of all the most popular container plants, but by choosing your favourites from these plants you will have made a good start in establishing a versatile and attractive container-grown garden.

Cacti and Other Succulents

Both cacti and succulents are plant groups which have adapted to dry conditions and are able to store water in their fleshy stems, leaves or branches. Cacti usually have no leaves, and very nearly all have spines, bristles or hairs. Their greatest asset is their unbelievably beautiful flowers. Succulents include such diverse plants as crassulas, euphorbias, hoyas, and many others, which come from different families, many of them boasting leaves with a sculptured look. Cacti and other succulents generally have shallow roots, therefore most take well to container planting.

Growth habits

Cacti and succulents include a wealth of plants of an amazing variety of form. *Aloe barberiae (A. bainesii)* resembles a small tree, the echinocactus species look like a football covered with lethal spikes, some kalanchoe species have flannel-like leaves, while lithops exactly resemble the stones around them.

There are also many spectacular architectural plants, such as the agaves (*see* p. 68), which, with their rosettes of large leaves, will be a feature on their own or create a focal point in a group, especially if planted in an interesting pot. But not only these giants are of interest. Many cacti and suc-

culents, such as haworthias and lithops, are small enough to fit into very small individual containers, or may be planted together, interspersed with pebbles, to create a dish garden. Trailing species, such as stapelias, will cascade over the edge of a container. Other trailing species are *Crassula perfoliata*, ceropegias, epiphyllums, zygocactus, *Aporocactus flagelliformis* and echeverias.

Suitable containers

When choosing containers for cacti and succulents, the shape and growth form of the plants must be borne in mind. Large pots or urns are suitable for plants with strong forms, such as the agaves, while low-growing species, such as sempervivums, mammillarias, notocactus and lobivias, and creeping species, such as rhombophyllums, lampranthus, drosanthemums, sedums and stapelias, will look more at home in a wide, shallow container.

Hanging baskets are ideal for displaying the many striking trailing species, such as echeverias, sedums, stapelias, ceropegias, epiphyllums and zygocactus, while larger tubs or long troughs can be planted with a variety of tall, spreading and trailing plants.

These containers of good scale lend height to an interesting collection of succulents, including echeverias, kalanchoes, sedums and bryophyllums.

General growing conditions

Most succulents do best in dry, sunny conditions and need to be protected against too much rain and waterlogged conditions. Generally they are not well suited to moist, humid regions, or to areas experiencing heavy frost.

It is difficult to generalize on soil mixes, except to say that they simply must be well drained. A good mix is one of garden soil, compost and coarse sand, the cacti needing more sand.

Planting and routine care

They will need water from early spring through to autumn, when the soil is dry, and at the end of autumn the water can be cut down to allow them to have a winter rest.

If plants are to be moved, leave them to dry out for a day or so, so that the damaged roots do not rot. If it is planted straight away, the roots, which are still fleshy, will tend to rot if they come into contact with water.

Larger plants may need a light dressing of fertilizer during the growing season.

Plants have to be repotted when the nutrients in the soil have been depleted or when their roots have filled the pot. Before lifting a plant, allow the soil to dry out. To lift a spiny cactus, make a roll of newspaper, flatten it, and wrap this around the plant, leaving enough paper so the two ends may be brought together, as a handle. Repot as explained on p. 121.

Choosing the plants

Group plants with interesting foliage and different flowering periods for a lasting display of colour and structure. A tall *Euphorbia candelabrum* with perhaps just one side stem, or a tall cactus (cephalocereus) for height, with echinocacti in a group, interplanted with sedums or *Kalanchoe blossfeldiana*, and rhipsalis cascading over the edge, will make a striking display in a large container. Try *Aeonium arboreum* as a centrepiece, with *Kalanchoe tubiflora* around it. Then plant lower-growing *Kalanchoe tomentosa* with *Sedum rubrotuncum*, with a row of haworthias around the edge.

The echeveria species, with their colourful rosettes of fleshy leaves in green, red or purple, and their sprays of red or orange bell-shaped flowers, are often planted on their own in flat containers or hanging baskets. The basket should be on the large size, with strong chains or wire to support it. Line it with plastic and fill with soil, and push stems of echeveria through slits in the plastic all the way round and also plant them in the soil surface. As they grow, they will compete for light, and in a fairly short time, a perfectly symmetrical sphere will have formed.

Aloes come in a large range of sizes and most will happily grow in containers. A single *Aloe africana*, or *A. candelabra* in a container with a natural look (such as terracotta or an ethnic pot), placed in a hot, sunny part of the patio, will create its own splendour without the company of other plants. The variegated leaves of the tiny *A. variegata* will make an interesting display if several plants surround a tall-growing, green cactus, such as echinocereus or cephalocereus.

Succulents that will mix with other plants include the jade plant *(Crassula arborescens)*, which has a bushy growth and rosettes of leaves of dark purple, and the aeonium species, which don't mind growing in the shade, and bear attractive rosettes of leaves on sturdy stems.

Other succulents which will grow in the shade are the Easter cactus *(Rhipsalidopsis gaertneri)* and Christmas cactus *(Schlumbergera x buckleyi)* with their spectacular flowers, as well as the epiphyllum and the zygocactus species. Epiphyllums have long flat stems, and large, trumpet-shaped flowers of brilliantly coloured satin, while the stems of zygocactus are shorter, with irregularly shaped flowers. They thrive with surprisingly little attention, and will take to hanging baskets, or to being planted in containers with an extremely loose, well-drained soil mixture.

Cacti and succulents with dangerous spines or spiky leaves should never be placed on a well-trafficked patio or in areas where children play, however interesting they may be to collectors.

Conifers

There is such a huge diversity of conifer varieties that it is no wonder that gardeners throughout the country are using them extensively not only in the garden, but also for container planting.

With colours ranging from various shades of green through clear gold to grey-green with a purple tinge, conifers can blend or contrast with other plants, or make a colourful group on their own. You can use the bright yellows and silvers for contrast, and the many shades of green for background colour. Many conifers have the added advantage of changing colour in winter, which makes them extremely valuable in the cold months, when little else is in bloom. Add to this the fact that very nearly all conifers are frost hardy, and that their shapes are many and varied, and it will be obvious why they are among the most valued of container plants.

Growth habits

There are tall and slender varieties such as *Cupressus sempervirens* "Swane's Gold" and the silvery *Juniperus scopolorum* "Skyrocket", conical shapes such as *Platycladus orientalis* "Golden Rocket", short and fat varieties such as the yellow and gold *Thuja occidentalis* "Rheingold", and those with a spreading habit, such as *Juniperus conferta* and *J. horizontalis*, suitable as a groundcover or for cascading over a container.

Containers and combinations

On the whole, tall, slender conifers look better in tall pots, whereas the lower-growing types are

Above: White pebbles add the finishing touch to this contained conifer.

Left: The euphorbia is an unusual contrast to the rounded form of the jars and decoration.

Above: A Mediterranean look is created by white walls and white pots planted with conifers and asparagus.

Right: A charming trio of small "Goldcrest" conifers in sturdy concrete pots defines the entrance to a flight of steps.

better suited to the flatter containers. As a general rule the size of the container should be about a third of the overall height of the tree at maturity.

Generally, there is no limit to the scope of container-grown conifers and they can even be planted in windowboxes.

Three dwarf conifers, such as "Rheingold", combined with trailing ivy, can create a most interesting effect in a windowbox. A single specimen such as "Gold Crest" or "Donard Gold" surrounded by brightly flowering begonias is an elegant foil for their abundance of colour.

A container grouping consisting of a variety of conifers is most attractive. Group a variety of different shapes, sizes and colours in an open corner: choose a tall, dense-growing type, such as "Golden Rocket" or *Chamaecyparis lawsonia* "Winston Churchill" as focal point, surrounded by other shapes and different colours, for instance *Juniperus horizontalis* "Plumosa", *Davurica expansa* "Variegata" and *Chamaecyparis lawsonia* "Tamariscifolia".

A row of conifers of the same variety along a wall or the driveway will add grace and elegance, as will those which are placed on either side of a door or gate, or on each of a series of steps. Or place a conifer of substantial growth and shape on either side of a statue.

General growing conditions

Most conifers prefer a place in the sun, but some will grow in the shade, such as the *Juniperus conferta*, which will create a groundcover in shade or semi-shade.

Soil must be organically rich, and, most important, well drained. Commercial potting soil to which a handful of bone meal has been added will suffice, and regular application of liquid sea manure followed by a good soaking will keep them in good health.

Planting and routine care

Pruning should not be necessary, except to keep them in good shape, but it may be necessary to take out dead or straggling, woody growth, and this should be cut right back to the main stem. Some conifers are particularly suitable for topiary, for instance "Swane's Gold", "Goldcrest" and *Platycladus orientalis* varieties.

Conifers should only be repotted when it is absolutely necessary, when roots become overcrowded (*see* p. 121).

A tall-growing conifer may have to be staked to keep it upright until its trunk is sufficiently sturdy to make it self-supporting.

• Conifers for Containers •

Spreading: *Juniperus horizontalis* "Wiltonii" is slow growing with blue-green foliage turning purple in winter. *J. davurica* "Expansa Variegata" has a flat growth habit, and is slow growing with cream-coloured leaves scattered over the grey-green foliage. *J. x media* "Prince of Wales" is slow growing and has clear green foliage that takes on a purple tint in winter. *J. procumbens* "Nana" is slow growing with yellow-green foliage. *J. horizontalis* "Plumosa" is slow growing and has fine grey-green foliage turning purple in autumn and winter.

Pencil-shaped: *Juniperus scropulorum* "Skyrocket" is fairly slow growing with a very narrow, upright growth habit and blue-grey foliage. *Cupressus sempervirens* "Swane's Gold" is fairly slow growing. With its tidy, compact growth and golden-yellow foliage it is one of the best container plants. *C. sempervirens* (Italian cypress) has dark green foliage and is well-known for its upright, slender growth. It will tolerate hot, humid conditions.

Conical: *Chamaecyparis pisifera* "Boulevard" is slow growing, but with its dense, silvery foliage is among the most popular conifers. *C. obtusa* "Crippsii" (golden cypress) is one of the faster growers. It has an open habit and attractive golden yellow foliage which makes it one of the old favourites. *Juniperus squamata* "Loderii" is slow growing, but its compact shape and grey-green foliage make it an excellent container subject. *J x media* "Blaauw" is a slow grower with ascending branches – the tips of the branches pointing upwards. It has deep bluish-green foliage throughout the year.

Globose: *Thuja occidentalis* "Sunkist Gold" is slow growing with a rounded form and attractive gold-kissed foliage. "Hetz Midget" is a true dwarf. This slow-growing conifer forms a compact bush and its dark green foliage turns bronze in autumn.

Rounded: *Chamaecyparis lawsonia* "Tamariscifolia" is also known as the bird's nest conifer. It is slow growing and has greyish-green, flat, fern-like foliage. "Minima Aurea" is slow growing and forms a squat, almost rounded bush, with rich golden foliage all year round. *Thuja occidentalis* "Woodwardii" is slow growing with strong stems. Its green foliage turns bronze in autumn. "Rheingold" has an open habit and is slow growing, with bright green foliage changing to rich gold and bronze in autumn and to more intense colours in winter.

Pyramid: *Thuja occidentalis* "Smaragd" is another slow grower. "Smaragd" is the Russian word for "emerald" which accurately describes the rich, green foliage of this attractive conifer which, with its neat and compact growth, is one of the best and most popular container subjects. *Cupressus macrocarpa* "Silver Queen" is slow growing with silver-grey foliage.

Upright: *Platycladus orientalis* "Aurea Nana" is slow growing. Its golden foliage changes to a deeper golden colour in winter and it makes an excellent container plant.

Compact: *Cryptomeria japonica* "Vilmoriniana" is a slow growing dwarf conifer with vivid green foliage turning purple in winter, and a neat, compact growth. *Platycladus orientalis* "Compacta" is slow growing

This nandina and a "Rheingold" conifer have both taken on a natural spherical shape in their pebble clad pots, making for an attractive, harmonious combination.

with shining green foliage all year round. "Aurea Nana Compacta" is a slow-growing conifer and forms a compact, roundish bush. The golden-green foliage of this popular container plant changes to a rich golden colour in winter.

Columnar: *Platycladus orientalis* "Elegantissima" is fairly fast growing, with vertically flattened foliage of bright green turning a rich bronze colour in winter. "Golden Rocket" grows fairly fast and its rocket shape makes it an excellent accent plant in a container. Its bright green foliage turns rich, golden-bronze in winter. *Chamaecyparis lawsoniana* "Columnaris" is fairly slow growing, but may eventually outgrow its pot. It has densely packed foliage of bluish green. *Cupressus macrocarpa* "Donard Gold" is a fast grower with rich golden-yellow foliage all year round. It will become too large for a container after a few years, when it can be planted into the garden.

A pleasing combination of beautiful terracotta containers on a large scale house a variety of conifers and acers, breaking up a wide expanse of brick paving. This is backed by "Goldcrest" conifers, with a groundcover of juniper in the foreground.

Fuchsias

These charmers have a large following among gardeners who are attracted by their single or double flowers of many rich colours, as well as more subtle tones, some with very full skirts. They come into new growth in spring and bear their flowers through to early autumn.

As their flowers have a hanging habit, fuchsias are ideal for hanging baskets, where they may be looked up to, and for windowboxes. For this reason they are welcomed onto the patio and areas around the house, where their spectacular flowers can be admired.

Container-grown fuchsias are a lovely part of the summer garden. Standards placed among annuals and perennials in a mixed border will

A large hanging basket lined with coir and plastic is generously planted with a fuchsia, lobelia and pansies.

Overleaf: Buckets, pots and baskets of colourful fuchsias and impatiens in mid-summer.

MAKING A STANDARD

The making of a standard starts with a cutting, which must be straight. As it is planted in its pot, drive a straight stake into the pot, close to the cutting, for future support. Allow the cutting to grow, continually supporting it by tying it to the stake and gently rubbing off any side stems, but keeping the top leaves. Once the stem has reached the required height, which may be from 60 cm to 1,5 m, pinch out the central growth to prevent the stem from growing upwards and to encourage side growth. Pinch back the terminal buds of these side stems two to three times to ensure a bushy shape before allowing the flowers to develop. Soil conditions, feeding, watering and pruning will now be the same as for a bush fuchsia.

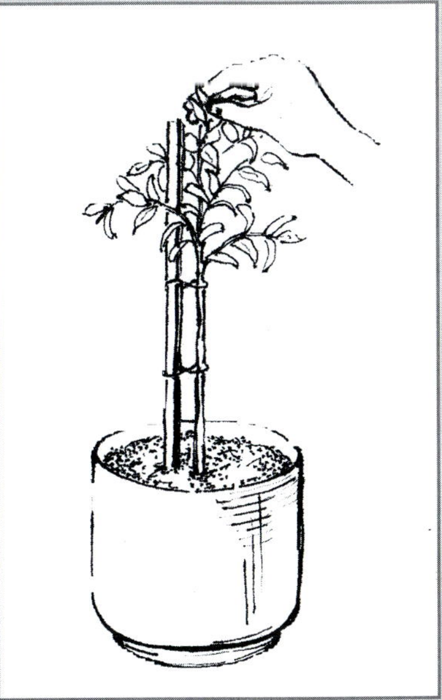

lend height and their added colour will bring about a festive air. In the high shade of trees container-grown fuchsias will look lovely if placed close together and interspersed with potted ferns. They mix well with plants such as aspidistra, chlorophytums, impatiens, hostas and begonias and *Campanula carpatica.*

Growth habits

Generally, the cascading fuchsia varieties are best suited to container planting, although an upright shrub or a fuchsia standard also looks good, especially if accompanied by smaller plants such as low-growing ferns or impatiens, or groundcovers such as callisia and lamium.

Among the best cascading varieties are "Bobby Boy", with red tubes and sepals and double purple corolla (petals); "Joan Pacey" of two delicate shades of pink; "Auntie Jinks", with red tubes and sepals and mauve corolla, and "Caroline" with pink tubes and sepals and mauve corolla.

"Lindissima" is another cascading variety with red tubes and sepals and very full, double creamy-pink corolla.

Good fuchsias that can be trained as standards are "Marinka" which is red all over, and "Citation" with pink tubes and sepals and pink veining in its white corolla.

General growing conditions

The best aspect is one which receives the morning sun. Fuchsias will also thrive in all-day semi-shade, but certainly not in deep shade. The high shade of a tree is ideal.

Full sun all day will burn the flowers and strong wind will damage them; this should be borne in mind when you decide on their position. Fuchsias will not take heavy frost, but as their flowering period is over before winter when they become dormant and can be moved, this does not really matter.

Fuchsias need well-drained, rich and friable soil with plenty of organics such as well-rotted compost and/or kraal manure. Add pine bark to ensure good drainage, and one teaspoon of superphosphate to each litre of soil.

During the growing season, extra food will be necessary to keep the growth healthy, together with abundant water.

Planting and routine care

For hanging baskets, use up to three small plants, depending on the size of the basket, but stick to the same cultivar as different cultivars grow at different rates. Line the basket with moss, fill with soil and insert the plants, facing outwards, around the rim of the basket.

Fuchsias bear their flowers at the stem ends, and with this in mind, to make for a compact bushy growth, all stem ends should be pinched back in their early growth. This will encourage more stems to grow which, in turn, can also be pinched back. This procedure can be carried out at least three times, before allowing the stems to develop, and bloom.

Once the plants are growing well in the new season, having developed a good foliage and showing the desired compact, bushy growth, they can be given slow-release fertilizer at the

Above: "Caroline" is a popular single fuchsia.

Below: "Lindissima" is a bountiful bloomer.

rate recommended on the packaging, followed by a thorough soaking.

Fuchsias must be kept damp all through the growing season, and during hot, dry spells, those in baskets and fairly small containers should be watered once a day. Under such conditions fuchsias may sometimes take on a wilted look despite having been well watered, but they will recover with the cool of the evening.

In frost-free areas, fuchsias are best pruned in July. In areas experiencing moderate frost, leave this chore until spring. Cut back the new season's growth to two or three buds. Pruning should always be followed by a dressing of general or special fertilizer, a thorough drenching, plus a good layer of mulch.

Cuttings strike easily. Take tip cuttings of about 10 cm, remove the lower leaves, and plant into damp, coarse sand in small pots. Transplant the fuchsias into larger pots as soon as a good root system has developed.

A festival of colour is brought about by impatiens, hydrangeas, begonias and roses, the wall-mounted container acting as a focal point.

Ferns

No garden should be without at least a few ferns, and as they grow obligingly well in containers, they can be used in many parts of the garden where their foliage will add texture and create a luxuriant look.

A group of container-grown ferns on the patio, or in a shady spot in the garden, will have a cool, green impact. Being good mixers, they can be planted among other shade-loving container plants such as fuchsias and begonias. Those with long fronds placed on a pedestal among other bedding plants will lend welcome height and take up less floor space. Ferns also make excellent accent plants, showing off their striking leaf

forms. A large, healthy asplenium (bird's nest fern) placed on a pedestal overlooking other ferns, will create a striking accent, as would a platycerium (staghorn fern).

Growth habits

There is a huge selection of ferns to choose from, from the gigantic tree ferns to the indigenous *Blechnum australe* and the lower growing maidenhairs. The tree fern is the tallest, with its strong trunk and very long fronds, and makes a good accent plant.

Ferns not only come in greatly differing sizes – their fronds may also take on different shapes. The asplenium (bird's nest fern) has broad, straplike leaves which hardly resemble a fern, and the pellaea has circular fronds which look like leaves. An unusual fern is the epiphytic *Platycerium bifurcatum,* (staghorn fern) with its flat plates and long fronds.

Indigenous ferns, such as *Adiantum pedatum* (common maidenhair), *Blechnum australe* (South African fern), *Cyathea capensis* (forest tree fern), *C. dregei* (common tree fern), *Dryopteris spp.* and *Rumohra adiantiformis* (Knysna or leather fern), may not be taken from their wild habitat, but are available from nurseries and are all suitable container subjects.

General growing conditions

Ferns prefer a light, loose soil mix, rich in organic material: try two parts good, rich loam, one part compost or well-rotted kraal manure, one part leafmould and one part sand. To each 25 litres of this add half a cup of bone meal and half a cup of slow-release fertilizer.

All ferns like warm, damp conditions, and most of them are tender to frost, which makes it almost essential, in frosty areas, to plant them in containers which can be moved around. Alternatively, place their containers in a sheltered position.

Ferns grow best in shade or semi-shade, except for the indigenous common tree fern *(Cyathea dregei)*, which will tolerate sun provided that the soil is kept moist.

Planting and routine care

Ferns can be planted into containers any time of the year, but try to avoid very hot or very cold conditions. Make sure that the container selected is big enough to accommodate the fern's root system and plant the fern with its crown flush to the surface.

After planting, regular applications of liquid manure every three weeks will ensure lush, healthy growth.

Ferns need copious amounts of water and although they must never be allowed to become waterlogged, they should be kept moist at all times. A good mulching of compost or leaf mould will help to retain moisture.

Replace the top soil once a year with rich compost or leaf mould and regularly remove dead fronds to encourage new growth.

Centre: Ferns, planted and in hanging baskets, together with two fine specimens of furcraea in spectacular oriental pots create a luxuriant, subtropical effect in this covered pool area.

Overleaf: A symphony of green ferns with touches of colour creates a peaceful haven in a shady corner of a patio.

Below: An unusual colour combination of burgundy cordyline and a golden sword fern.

• *Ferns for Containers* •

Tree ferns. The fast-growing Australian tree fern *(Cyathea australis)* will grow well in a good-sized pot, the height of which should allow the long fronds to be displayed at their best. Place it near a water feature for a lovely effect. If planted into a sufficiently large container, a woodland "garden" can be created by underplanting it with maidenhair and leather ferns. It cannot take heavy frost, but can be moved to a sheltered place when it dies down in winter. Water well all through spring and summer, reducing the water in autumn. The best way to water is to saturate its trunk from the top. A newly planted tree fern needs this treatment every two or three days until its roots are established, then once a week. Apply liquid sea manure every two weeks around the base of the trunk.

Maidenhair ferns. Surely the most popular of ferns is the maidenhair *(Adiantum spp.)* with its fine, heart-shaped or rounded, mist-green leaves. The common maidenhair fern *(A. aethiopicum)* is indigenous to southern Africa. It needs an organically rich soil, and once the new growth starts in early spring, it should be watered well and regularly, with added misting in hot dry weather. When the growth is full, give it liquid manure once a week. If the growth is dense, and in need of division, take out the entire plant, and cut through it to divide it into two or four separate pieces, each of which can then be replanted into new soil. Maidenhairs are happy mixers, with fuchsias, streptocarpus, hostas, impatiens, plectranthus, dieffenbachias or aglaoenema. They may also be used to underplant taller aspleniums and blechnums.

Sword ferns *(Nephrolepis cordifolia)* come in several forms, some erect, some weeping and some with very fine leaves. They are most obliging, growing well in

baskets and other containers. Hang baskets from tree branches, or on the patio, and give them plenty of water: at all times in warmer regions, and all through spring and summer in more temperate gardens. Regular feeding with special fern food, slow-release potplant food or liquid manure, and a dressing of bone meal twice a year, will keep their fronds healthy. Sword ferns spread at a great rate and need to be kept in check by regularly removing weak growth and spent fronds. It is advisable to keep them in their own pots and submerge these into large containers where other plants have been planted. Their cascading form makes them suitable for planting at the edge of large containers under tall dieffenbachias, codiaeums, acalyphas or cordylines.

Staghorn ferns *(Platycerium spp.)* are always a talking point, whether they are in a container or in a basket. They have two kinds of leaves – those which form a shield of green, which wraps itself around a pot, and those with enormously long fronds which resemble stags' horns. Water and food should be placed into the centre of the shield growth, the food consisting of liquid manure. Some growers swear by feeding their staghorn ferns on banana peels. Regular sprayings with foliar feed will keep the plant in good condition.

Rabbit's foot *(Davallia pyxidata)* has furry rhizomes or creeping stems, with fine, lacy fronds and is a popular choice for hanging baskets. It is difficult to find suitable company for davallia because of its habit of forming a thick mat of rhizomes, but if it is planted at the edge of a container with a fuchsia standard in the centre, any surplus inner growth can be removed.

Blechnums. The *Blechnum spp.*, the Norfolk Island fern and the South African fern, have broad fronds resembling fishbones and grow on a single stem. *B. gibbum*, the miniature tree fern, has an attractive crown of finely divided fronds and is an excellent container plant in temperate and sub-tropical regions. Leave space in their container for maidenhairs, or surround them with selaginella or soleirolia.

Hardy ferns. *Dicksonia antarctica* (the soft tree fern) is a hardy, frost-resistant species with an attractive, spreading crown of dark green fronds reaching a length of up to 1,5 m. Another hardy species is *Dryopteris bergiana* which may reach a height of almost a metre. It has a short, stubby crown of long, pinnate leaves, closely resembling a tree fern.

The dainty maidenhair fern is an excellent leafy subject for a shaded windowbox or a shady spot on the patio.

Bird's nest ferns *(Asplenium nidus)* have broad, shiny, olive-green leaves and will tolerate mild frost. It needs extremely good drainage, so add pine bark chips to the soil mix. It makes a splendid sight on its own, and will always be a focal point in a grouping. Give it groundcovers such as tradescantia or callisia.

Round-leafed fern. As indicated by its name, the round-leafed fern *(Pellaea rotundifolia)* has small, round "leaves". The fronds are dark green above and light green beneath, which gives this fern an interesting variegated look. It is a low-growing fern, tolerant of full sun as long as it is kept moist, and easy to grow. With its long, narrow fronds it looks particularly attractive in hanging baskets, or as a groundcover surrounding flowering standards or calamondin.

Holly fern *(Cyrtomium falcatum)*. The glossy, green fronds of the holly fern grow in a rosette shape, creating the impression of rectangular leaves. It has a luxuriant look and is as attractive in a basket as in a pot mixed with other ferns, impatiens, fuchsias or hostas.

Hydrangeas

Hydrangeas bring a feast of summer colour to the garden and grow exceptionally well in containers. Tubs filled with hydrangeas will add their quota of beauty and interest to any patio or sitting-out area.

Most nurseries have a good selection of named varieties of hydrangeas, and it is certainly worthwhile investing in these, as they will have a strong growth, and their flower heads will be of a good size and shape.

Colour

It is a well-known fact that the colour of the flowers depends on the pH of the soil in which the plants grow, and the biggest advantage of container-grown hydrangeas is that you can control this. An acid soil will give blues, and an alkaline soil will give pinks. But this is not the whole story: if the soil is made too alkaline, leaves will suffer, and turn yellow. If your soil is slightly alkaline, add half a teaspoon of aluminium sulphate to five litres of water. Use this every ten days until the flowers have developed, which should have a blue tinge. There are also special products on the market which will affect the colour of your hydrangeas.

There are varieties which tend towards either pink or blue. "Daphne" is a vibrant red, a colour it will keep in acid soil, whereas "Apollo" will be bluer in acid soil, deep pink in alkaline soil. "Queen Mary" with its large heads of flowers with serrated petals, will be pale blue in acid soil, and pale pink in alkaline soil.

Opposite: "Queen Mary" bears well-shaped heads of flowers which may be blue or pink depending on the soil conditions.

Containerized hydrangeas must have copious amounts of water during their growing season.

Growth habits

The common hydrangea *(Hydrangea macrophylla)*, also called Christmas flowers owing to its flowering period, has large, toothed leaves and bears large, round flowerheads in white, pinks and blues in summer through autumn.

The lace-cap hydrangea, a variety of the common hydrangea, as well as the peegee hydrangea *(H. paniculata* "Grandiflora") and the oak-leafed hydrangea *(H. quercifolia)* are not really suited to container planting.

The climbing hydrangea *(H. petiolaris)* is a deciduous, self-clinging climber with attractive, finely toothed oval leaves, bearing flattened heads of small white flowers in summer. It may be too vigorous for container planting.

General growing conditions

Hydrangeas need rich, well-drained soil. A good mixture of top soil and compost will be beneficial, and where soil is alkaline, it would be advisable to use acid compost, which is available from all nurseries. A mulch will help to retain moisture, and keep the soil cool.

As they bloom during the hottest months of the year, hydrangeas are best planted in semi-shade, but not deep shade, which will result in pale flowers. They will also do well in a position which receives morning sun. A sunny position is ideal where humidity is fairly high, and they will thrive in filtered shade on the patio or in the shade of tall-growing trees.

Hydrangeas need protection from strong summer winds, notably from the south easter in the Western Cape.

Planting and routine care

As container-grown hydrangeas have a limited amount of soil, they need regular feeding to ensure healthy growth and abundant flowers. After planting, give the plant a good drenching, and when it is growing well, from late spring, give it regular doses, every ten days, of liquid sea manure, *Nitrosol* or other slow-release fertilizers according to the instructions on the packaging.

Hydrangeas need copious amounts of water during summer when they grow and bloom, and frequent watering is of the utmost importance. Once a week, or even more frequently in very hot, dry weather, give your container-grown hydrangeas enough water to flow through the soil until it emerges from the drainage holes. Repeat this once or twice more to ensure an adequate water supply. Leaves and flowers of plants allowed to dry out never recover completely and

are often marked with brown edges. Leaves turning yellow may be a sign of trace-element deficiency. Add 6 g of sulphate of iron to 5 litres of water and give this to the affected plant once a week until the green returns, or apply a commercial product.

Prune container-grown hydrangeas in winter, except in areas experiencing heavy frost, where pruning is best left until spring. Cut flowering stems to where there are two healthy buds, from which two healthy new stems will arise. Unflowered stems should be left. This method will result in a lot of flowers, but if you want long stems with large flowers, it is better to cut every stem to the lowest buds. Hydrangeas pruned in this way will take longer to reach full growth and they will bloom later.

In spring, the top 2,5 cm of soil should be replaced with well-enriched compost, followed by a good layer of mulch.

Combinations

Hydrangeas planted in wooden wine barrels or large terracotta pots can be underplanted with brightly flowering annuals, such as alyssum, begonias and *Primula malacoides*. In a large, round container, plant a blue hydrangea in the centre, surround it with bright blue torenias and plant white alyssum around the edge.

In the shade, hydrangeas combined with fuchsias, dieffenbachias and other foliage plants will put on a good display. Impatiens and hydrangeas are both summer bloomers and make a good combination with trailing vinca tumbling over the edge of the container.

Palms

Palms bring with them an air of the exotic, of tranquil lagoons far away. They make excellent accent plants in containers, and most palms, especially the slower-growing varieties, take extremely well to container planting.

Growth habits

Some palms have a single trunk, others have a cluster of trunks, but each trunk has the same characteristics. Firstly, there are no side branches, and there is only one terminal leaf, which means that if this leaf and the top growth on a trunk is destroyed, there will be no further growth and the trunk will eventually die. Furthermore, damage to a trunk will not be healed by scar tissue, but will form an unsightly cavity.

The roots of palms form a thick, fibrous mat which is wider than deep, with no tap roots. This mat of roots should be kept moist at all times and watered regularly through spring and summer.

General growing conditions

Palms relish warm, humid conditions and will be at their best in the sub-tropical areas, such as the Natal coast, where magnificent avenues of palms are to be seen, and the selection is the greatest for both garden and container-grown palms. But there is a wide range of palms to choose from,

Opposite: The bamboo palm needs a surprisingly small container to grow big and tall.

Far left: A bamboo palm and a miniature date palm combine well with other warm climate plants to create a serene atmosphere.

Left: Ferns, dieffenbachias, dracaenas and palms in white containers create a cool green corner on a tiled patio.

Overleaf: In a frost-free garden potted palms are surrounded by bromeliads, philodendrons, crotons and other tropical plants.

and several varieties will thrive in containers outside in all regions of the country.

Many palms can tolerate a certain amount of cold and some can even take heavy frost. A sudden drop in temperature can be highly damaging, however, and where winters are very severe, it is better to place palms in a sheltered position on the patio, or in containers which can be moved indoors at night.

Most palms need good light, although they can tolerate poor light for a short time.

The soil should be rich and porous, with excellent drainage. A good mix would be one part good garden loam, one part compost or well-rotted kraal manure, and one part coarse, clean sand, with a handful of bone meal to every 25 litres of soil.

Planting and routine care

Palms have spreading surface roots, and containers selected should allow for this. They can be planted throughout the year, although spring is the best time. Water thoroughly after planting.

Palms need regular feeding and watering to keep their magnificent foliage in the best possible shape. Feed your palms regularly through spring and summer with 3:2:1 – 60 g to every square metre of surface every six weeks, followed by a good soaking. Alternatively, use a slow-release fertilizer or liquid manure.

Watering is extremely important as the fibrous roots soon dry out. During hot, dry weather, it may be necessary to water container-grown palms every two or three days.

The greatest care must be taken to ensure that the water does not collect around the roots, as a waterlogged condition for any length of time will cause them to rot. A good layer of mulch will help to keep the roots cool.

Grouping and combinations

Groups of palms, each in its own container, of different heights and shapes, can be brought together where the wind is not too strong. To add to the tropical look they should be given the company of philodendrons, *Monstera deliciosa*, *Strelitzia nicolai* and bougainvilleas. In the subtropical parts crotons, acalyphas, anthuriums and marantas will complete the picture.

As most pool areas are enclosed and secluded, conditions are often much warmer than in other areas. This is where palms will come to their best, provided they are given adequate water and are kept moist, but not waterlogged, at all times.

• *Palms for Containers* •

Frost-hardy palms include the following: *Trachycarpus fortunei* (Chinese windmill palm) is the most cold resistant. It has a tall, slender trunk with large fan leaves, and tolerates both dense shade and full sun. *Chamaerops humilis* (European fan palm) tolerates widely divergent climatic conditions. *Washingtonia filifera* (petticoat palm) is a tall-growing palm with a beard of dead fronds immediately below the crown of fan-shaped fronds, resembling a petticoat. *Washingtonia robusta* (cotton palm) grows tall, with bright green fan-like leaves. *Livistona chinensis* (Chinese fan palm) has a thick trunk with large, fan-shaped glossy green leaves. It tolerates moderate frost in a warm, sheltered position. *Butia capita* (jelly palm) has blue-green foliage on long, drooping spines and is a most decorative container plant. It thrives in sub-tropical conditions but is surprisingly hardy in cold conditions.

Light to moderate frost: The following palms will tolerate light to moderate frost: *Sabal minor* (dwarf palmetto) has huge, blue-green, fan-like fronds. It is slow-growing and cold-hardy, growing well in full sun. It is a good container plant for the poolside in cooler areas. *Rhapis excelsa* (lady palm) is a multi-stemmed palm, slow-growing, and fairly tolerant of cold, but not direct sun. Its very dark green fronds are widely spaced and erect. It forms a dense clump and looks particularly attractive in a container. *Phoenix roebelenii* (miniature date palm) looks lovely on a light and bright patio, but its spiny fronds need lots of space. It will grow in full sun in the garden, but needs adequate moisture. *Phoenix canariensis* (Canary island palm) is a fairly hardy, elegant plant with an upright-growing stem and a heavy head of plume-like fronds. *Phoenix reclinata* (wild date palm) is an elegant tree with long, plume-like fronds on a slender trunk. Plant this attractive palm in a tub, surrounded with brightly flowering annuals. *Chamaedorea elegans* (parlour palm) is a dwarf palm which will not tolerate direct sunlight. It is wind tender and needs a shady, sheltered position outdoors. Seedlings of the parlour palm are generally sold as the so-called love palms. *Chrysalidocarpus lutescens* (golden bamboo) makes a very attractive container plant on the patio in dappled shade. It bears a crown of greenish-yellow feathery leaves on golden trunks.

Palms for the poolside: The following palms will do well at the poolside in warm regions: *Mascarena verschaffeltii* (spindle palm) has a tapering trunk which thickens at the top with a dense crown of arching golden-yellow fronds with grey-green leaflets. It needs a warm, sheltered position outdoors. *Licuala grandis* is slow growing, does not tolerate wind, and needs a warm, moist position. Place it in a sheltered position on the patio or by the poolside.

Other good container subjects are *Caryota mitis* (fish tail palm) whose clusters of closely packed stems give it a bushy appearance. It does best in light shade. *Chamaedorea seifritzii* (Seifritz palm) has slender, upright stems. It is one of the most sun tolerant palms. *Howea forsteriana* (sentry palm) is regarded by many as the best for container planting. It has a slender single trunk, and long, upwards-curving fronds. It will tolerate moderate frost in a warm, sheltered position.

Below: Butia, with its grey-green leaves, is tough and hardy.

Pelargoniums

Pelargoniums are bountiful bloomers and are the mainstays of container gardening. For generations gardeners have insisted on giving the name, "Geranium" to these brilliantly coloured flowers with their wide variety of leaf forms, which grow equally well in the garden and in containers. But nowadays people are becoming more aware of the correct names. Very briefly, the family Geranicae has several genera, including the geraniums and the pelargoniums. Geraniums (of which the indigenous *G. incanum* is the best known) bear flowers with five regular petals, all identical, whereas the flowers of pelargoniums have two petals on the upper side and three on the underside, with distinct markings. In South Africa there are many indigenous pelargoniums which were taken overseas and hybridized into beautiful colours and compact growth.

Growth habits

Pelargonium zonale, the zonal pelargoniums (geraniums) have a bushy growth, with attractive, often boldly marked leaves and generous blooms. Although the flowers of the scented

Centre: Ivy-leafed pelargonium and lobelias in happy profusion in a rather large container.

Right: Pelargoniums, lobelias and fuchsias thrive in a sheltered spot receiving morning sun.

pelargoniums, such as nutmeg-scented *P. x fragrans*, lemon-scented *P. crispum* and peppermint-scented *P. tomentosum* are less striking, they bring a lovely fragrance to the patio.

P. tonganense has a low, spreading habit with ivy-like leaves and bright red flowers. It grows in humid areas where other pelargoniums may not do well because of rust. *P. x domesticum* (regal pelargoniums) have an erect, bushy habit with slightly woody stems, while *P. peltatum*, the ivy-leafed pelargoniums, are trailing plants with stems often up to 1 m long.

General growing conditions

Pelargoniums grow well throughout the country, except where heavy frost is experienced, or in very humid regions where they may be prone to rust. They need a loose, rich, well-drained mixture of sand and compost, with a teaspoon of slow-release fertilizer added to each 15 cm of soil. Most pelargoniums are sun lovers, although the zonal pelargoniums, and some of the scented pelargoniums, will also do well in semi-shade. Virtually all pelargoniums are wind tender and need to be protected from prevailing winds.

Planting and routine care

As pelargoniums come into growth, they will need slightly more water, and, as the buds make their first appearance, give them some slow-release fertilizer to encourage blooming. In hot, humid areas, they are prone to rust, and should be sprayed with fungicide soon after they come into new growth in spring.

Any stems which take on a woody, leggy look, should be cut back to the main stem, and cuttings taken from the removed growth to keep up a constant supply of plants.

All pelargoniums can be cut back after their flowering period, and given extra food to encourage a good crop of foliage.

Pelargoniums need plenty of water when they are growing, from early spring, but they should never be overwatered. Water the plants only in dry conditions when they are in flower.

Weep holes are essential in any large brick container to ensure that plants such as these pelargoniums have excellent drainage and will not become waterlogged.

• Pelargoniums for Containers •

Unusual use has been made of a rather large tree stump by hollowing out the centre and planting it with trailing pelargoniums, drainage being no problem as excess water would simply seep away into the wood.

Right: This wicker basket was lined with aluminium foil to prevent the basket from rotting, then filled with three pelargoniums (F1 hybrids), each in its own pot.

Regal pelargoniums. Good container subjects include the startlingly beautiful regal pelargoniums with large serrated leaves and flowers with dark centres. They are sold as pot plants, and in containers outdoors, do better on the cool side of the patio.

The zonal pelargoniums, our well-known, well-loved "geraniums", are valued for their coloured leaves and appreciated for their colourful blooms of many shades, from purest white through various shades of pink and mauve to deep purple and rich scarlet. Although these sun lovers will tolerate dry conditions and even poor soil, they will do all the better for added nutrients.

The ivy-leafed pelargonium, whose leaves are free of hairs, has a cascading habit and is an ideal subject for windowboxes and hanging baskets. Some varieties have extremely attractive bi-coloured flowers: pink and white, crimson and white, and deep violet and purple. There are also many scented pelargoniums, such as rose scented, nutmeg, lemon and peppermint. The nutmeg-scented pelargonium, with grey-green leaves and almost white flowers, has a rather dainty growth which makes it a good container subject for a semi-shaded position. Rose and lemon-scented pelargoniums have indented leaves and will grow in full sun or semi-shade.

The F1 hybrids have good foliage, and bear huge heads of flowers of clear, rich colours. Seed is prohibitively expensive, which accounts for the high cost of seedlings, but their outstanding growth and flowering makes them a worthy addition to any container garden.

Combinations

Plant F1 hybrids in an urn on a pedestal, or in a windowbox accompanied by ivy-leafed pelargoniums, helichrysum, *Senecio maritima*, or vivid blue lobelias or white alyssum. Or plant them in a large, flat container on their own, or mixed with lobelias or alyssum cascading over the edge.

Zonal pelargoniums will grow in containers and baskets, combined with lobelias, felicias, or *Kalanchoe blossfeldiana*. Most striking of all is a combination of several zonal pelargoniums of different colours, placed in a large, flat container in full sun on the patio. Try a combination of pink ivy-leafed pelargonium, pink or mauve petunias, a few stems of ivy, two or three blue violas and trailing white lobelia. They will also trail prettily from a windowbox, together with ivy. Plant upright pelargoniums in the box and the trailers at the edge. Scented pelargoniums will make excellent companions for fragrant herbs such as lavender, bergamotte or rosemary.

Roses

There are few roses that will not grow in a container, except for rampant climbers and ramblers, and taller-growing hybrid teas which may look out of proportion. In fact, long ago, roses were only grown in half-drums or large concrete containers in sub-tropical gardens where termites were prevalent. But why plant roses in pots if they do so well in the ground? One good reason is that they can be placed where ground-planted roses will not do, such as on the patio, or where extra height is needed, or out in the garden where trees' roots may interfere with their growth. Containerized roses have a definite place in any garden, and, being moveable, they can be taken out of view when they are not looking their best.

There is a vast selection of roses available and it will pay any gardener to consult a rose nursery or a good rose catalogue to choose container subjects according to the height and shape of the bush, and the colour and size of the blooms.

Growth habits

Standard roses, with a long stem and bushy growth at the top, are highly suitable for container planting, as they can be underplanted with other roses or with annuals. Standard roses usually come in three sizes: 50 cm tall miniatures; 90 cm tall floribundas; and 1,3 m tall hybrid teas and weeping standards such as "Ballerina", "Sea Foam", "Iceberg", "Firefalls" and "Red Cascade". Bear in mind that a standard consists of a long stock to the terminal growth of which have been grafted several buds of the hybrid rose. It follows, then, that if the top growth is destroyed, the hybrid rose is destroyed.

Standard roses should be thoroughly staked to keep them upright and to prevent wind damage, and all side growth below the grafts should be removed as soon as it appears.

A standard "Flower Carpet" and "Little Pink Hedge", underplanted with daisies and lobelias.

Floribundas have a low-growing habit and are particularly popular container subjects as they are easy to grow, produce an abundance of flowers in large clusters, and flower for a long period. A large variety of hybrid teas is available in bush and standard form.

Climbers and ramblers, on the whole, will happily take to container planting except for those with a rampant growth, such as "Albertine", "Dorothy Perkins", "Macartney Rose", "Mermaid" and "Lamarque". A good container subject is "Paul's Scarlet".

Miniature roses are also highly suitable for container-planting. They are usually less than 60 cm high and come in a wide colour range. The taller varieties can be standardized with good effect. Groundcover roses have a spreading habit, with flowers resembling the smaller cluster roses.

General growing conditions

Roses like to be in the sun for most of the day, except for the hot afternoon sun, and the ideal position is where they receive full sun in the morning. While they can take sudden gusts of wind, they will not thrive in conditions which are constantly windy.

Pink and white miniature roses with skirts of blue lobelias in terracotta pots make a charming picture.

Good soil for container-grown roses could be a mixture of half commercial rose compost and half good, loamy garden soil, with a handful of bone meal added. Chemical fertilizer is not recommended, as there could be a danger of burning the roots.

Good commercial soil mixes are available for rose growing, and may be considered for container-grown roses. Good drainage is essential as roses need a lot of water, but they should never be allowed to become waterlogged.

Planting and routine care

Container-grown roses can be planted virtually any time of the year. They should be planted at the same depth as that of the bag or container in which they were bought, the bud union being just under the soil surface.

Any damaged roots should be cleanly cut back to healthy growth. A shallow basin can be made around the plant to retain water. Once the rose has been planted and well watered to settle it, it should be given a good layer of mulch. Newly planted container-grown roses should be watered every two to three days until the plants have settled.

Roses in containers are treated in much the same way as those in the ground. Pruning procedure is the same as for plants in the ground and involves the removal of any weak or old growth. Stems which are older than the previous season should be completely removed, and three or four main stems left, which can be cut back by about half.

After pruning, remove the surface soil to a depth of about 2,5 cm and replace this with well-rotted compost, a handful of 2:3:2, 2:3:1 or 5:1:5, followed by a good soaking and a good layer of mulch. No more food will be necessary until early spring when further dressings of fertilizer can be given every month until the end of autumn. Mulching must be kept up throughout the season.

Roses are renowned for their love of water, and, in the limited space of containers, must be watered more often than those in the ground. Once every day or two is often not too much in hot, dry conditions, but this requires excellent drainage, which should be checked constantly.

Containers

When choosing containers for roses, keep to simple shapes such as plain terracotta, tubs and half-barrels so that a too-ornate container will not detract from the beauty of the roses.

Miniature bushes and standards will grow in a 30 cm container, but if they are to be mixed with other plants, they will need a container of 50 or 60 cm. Hybrid teas will look good in half wine barrels of at least 75 cm across.

An interesting effect can be created by filling a large wicker basket with pots of miniature bushes. Place the basket on a sheltered windowsill or on a table on the patio.

Miniatures with a cascading habit can be planted in hanging baskets of at least 50 cm across. Among the good choices are "Rosy Hit", "Show 'n Tell", "Red Minimo" and "Green Ice".

Ideal for windowboxes are groundcover roses such as "Angelita", "Baby Love", "My Granny", "Pink Flower Carpet", "White Flower Carpet", "Pink Sunsation", "White Sunsation" and "Sweet Chariot", as well as any of the miniatures mentioned before.

Combinations

Standards will take well to an underplanting of bush miniatures or groundcover roses, or almost any annuals.

A few miniature standards in pots, with lower containers of shrub miniatures, make a charming sight on a patio or a paved area out in the garden. Weeping standards look splendid in fairly shallow containers, underplanted with other roses, or other plants.

Roses can be given companions in the form of annuals such as alyssum, lobelia or violas planted around the edge of the container. Many gardeners like to plant annuals with roses to see them through the barren time of the roses.

Floribunda standards can either be underplanted with miniatures, or with the so-called groundcover roses, such as "Flower Carpet" and "Pink Sunsation" or "White Sunsation", as well as a large variety of annuals such as alyssum, pansies, violas or lobelias.

A pretty idea is to plant miniature roses into plastic pots which have been painted in shades of pink, blue and mauve, to blend with the rose colours. In pink or mauve pots, plant "Lovely Rosamin", "Cupcake", "Fashion Parade", "Jennifer Joy" – all pink – or white miniatures such as "Lifestyle", "Starlight" or "Amoretta". Dark blue or dark green pots will show up red roses such as "Maidy Red", "Red Minimo", or "Red Rosamin"; coral and salmon roses such as "Charming Rosamin", "Coral Rosamin" or "Dreamy Parade", and yellow and gold roses such as "Lynn Gold", "Golden Piccolo" and "Yellow Parade". In fact, dark green will show up and enhance the colour of any rose.

An "Iceberg" tumbling over the edge of a container atop the pipe is joined by a climber of the same variety growing from its base.

Try planting the miniature standard "Just for You" with its crimson blooms, underplanted with bush miniatures of the same variety, interspersed with alyssum and blue lobelias. Or plant a standard "Millie Walters" with its charming pink blooms with bush-forms of "American Rose" interspersed with pink dianthus or white petunias.

Herbs in containers are both useful and decorative. Opposite: A calamondin makes a pretty addition to a herb garden.

CHAPTER 8

Edible Container Plants

Fruit, vegetables and herbs in containers are both decorative and useful. Many varieties are suitable for container planting, which means that even flat dwellers with balcony gardens can enjoy the challenge of producing a variety of edible plants from their contained garden. Containers may range from a single pot housing one herb plant, to a strawberry pot planted with strawberries or a selection of herbs, or large-scale containers in which a variety of herbs and vegetables has been planted.

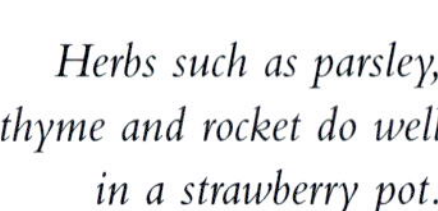

Herbs such as parsley, thyme and rocket do well in a strawberry pot.

Vegetables

In addition to being edible, vegetables provide interesting variations of shape and texture when combined with other plants in a container.

Growing conditions

Very nearly all vegetables need full sun for most of the day, so the siting of the containers is of vital importance. It may be tempting to place a well-planted container just outside the kitchen door, but this is not practicable if virtually no sun reaches it. The best site is one which receives sun for most of the day, except for the hot afternoon sun, which could be harmful to plants in a confined space. All need a well-dug, friable soil which has been enriched with plenty of organics, and general fertilizer. The soil must be well-drained and porous, but able to hold water.

Planting and routine care

For most vegetables, it works well to plant a succession at weekly or ten-day intervals, to keep up a fresh supply, bearing in mind the fact that some like warm growing conditions, for example beans, cucumbers and capsicum, while others, such as peas, carrots and lettuce, prefer a cooler climate. Container-grown vegetables will need plenty of nutrition, because regular watering and constant picking of the crops will take nutrients out of the soil. So give them an excellent start by

providing them with soil enriched with organics and general fertilizer.

Some vegetables, such as carrots, come to maturity and are then picked in their entirety, after which they are removed, and the soil is replenished. Others come to maturity, and produce their harvest over several weeks or even months – these include tomatoes, beans and capsicums, which must be kept well fed and watered throughout their productive period.

Vegetables planted in containers should be chosen for the abundance of their crop in proportion to their size, and their ability to be confined. Mixing and matching vegetables, or vegetables and herbs, can be fascinating, taking into account their height, their growth form, their leaves, and their colour, and naturally there will be times when some outgrow their neighbours. But this is all part of the experience, and the delight, of snipping off a lettuce for lunch, together with a few tomatoes and basil for garnish, or pulling some carrots for the soup, accompanied by herbs for taste. The following vegetables are suitable for container planting:

A large, dark green trough on the patio is an attractive host to a variety of herbs and vegetables, including mint, rosemary, thyme, marjoram, celery, leek and lettuce.

• Vegetables for Containers •

Beans *(Phaseolus spp.)* may be bushy or climbers, and are generous in their production. They will need added nitrogen, and plenty of water. Plant them in succession, three or four plants at a time, on the rim of a container, and place three or four long sticks in the form of a wigwam for them to climb up. Beans are warm-climate vegetables. Regular picking will prolong flowering and increase the crop.

Beetroots *(Beta vulgaris)* are often overlooked when it comes to vegetables, but they are highly useful as they can be picked when very young, and grated, their leaves can also be boiled and eaten, or eaten raw. Plant the seeds directly into the pot, and thin out the seedlings to about 10 cm apart. They can be planted all year in warm areas, and in spring in cold gardens.

Capsicums *(Capsicum spp.)* make attractive ornamental plants, and produce a good crop of shining green, red or yellow fruits which are full of goodness. Plant them in separate pots from spring onwards, and, when they are growing well, give them about a teaspoon of 2:3:2 followed by a good soaking. They will need plenty of water all through the season. Capsicums prefer a warmer climate, so plant them in summer in colder parts.

Carrots *(Daucus carota)* will need a good depth of soil – imagine a carrot, together with its long tip-root, and you will know the depth necessary. Plant several, about 5 cm apart, in a trough filled with plenty of compost or well-rotted kraal manure, as well as a sprinkling of 2:3:2. Keep them growing well with plenty of water, and pick them when they are young and tender. Growing them about six to a pot means that the entire pot can be picked, and with pots planted weekly, there will be constant a supply of carrots putting their pretty foliage on display. They can be planted all year in warm areas, but plant in spring in cooler parts. The first very young carrots may be harvested in as little as ten weeks.

Cucumbers *(Cucumis sativus)* may seem an unlikely subject for container planting, but if the young growth is pinched out twice, a more bushy growth, ideal for a container, will result. Plant a few plants in a long trough, and give them an attractive frame of metal or wood over which they can climb. They need warm growing conditions and copious watering, and prefer semi-shade. Start picking the cucumbers when they are very young.

For growing through winter, provide the containers with a "blind" of hessian or plastic, which can be drawn over them at night to protect the plants against frost. As a precaution against fungus pests, spray the plants with a good fungicide as soon as the leaves develop. Any plant suffering from wilt should be taken out and destroyed.

Lettuce *(Lactuca sativa)* have come into their own recently, with several new varieties, many of them highly decorative, with curled leaves, and leaves of rich colours. Plant them about 25 cm apart, water frequently, and make sure they come to maturity without any hold-ups. A layer of compost will keep their shallow roots cool. Plant a succession, and pick them from an early age. Some will even take kindly to having a few outer leaves picked at a time, while the rest of the

As well as being ornamental, marigolds help to ward off eelworm and other pests in the herb and vegetable garden.

plant is allowed to develop further. Lettuce prefer a cool growing season, but will grow in the warm season if given a little shade and plenty of water.

Marrows *(Curcubita pepo)* are delicious, and one vine will produce a good crop. They are usually picked young, then commonly known as zucchini, baby marrows or courgettes. Fill a container with organically enriched soil, make a small hillock in the centre, and plant several seeds in it. Thin out the seedlings to two or three, and give them a frame to climb over. Harvest regularly to encourage further flowering and fruiting. Marrows prefer warm conditions and a sheltered, sunny position.

Ornamental kale *(B. oleracea* var. *acephala).* Most cabbages grow large, and have a deep root system, which makes them less suitable for container planting, but the ornamental kale, which has colourful, interestingly shaped leaves, is highly decorative as well as highly nutritious. An almost continuous supply of water is necessary (*see also* p. 60).

Peas *(Pisum sativum)* are delicious when eaten raw or cooked, and even though they are not very productive in ratio to their size, it is worth growing a few, if there is space. Plant peas against a trellis to facilitate harvesting, and dust with a good fungicide.

Swiss chard *(Beta vulgaris* var. *cicla)* can look very handsome in a pot, and has the advantage that a few leaves may be removed at a time, which encourages further growth. It can be grown in virtually any climate and is very productive. Plants must be encouraged to develop and grow quickly for the best results. They need frequent watering and will benefit greatly from a permanent mulch. Cut flowering stems as soon as they form to stimulate further leaf development.

A large number of lettuce varieties are available with colours ranging from greenish yellow to deep burgundy.
Left: Ornamental or curly kale grows well in pots and can be eaten either cooked or raw, or used to garnish salads.

Tomatoes *(Lycopersicon esculentum)* are one of the most popular home-grown vegetables, giving an excellent crop for the amount of space they occupy. The attractive cherry tomatoes are very easy to grow, and can even be planted in hanging baskets. They will also cover a frame. Tomatoes need a good, rich soil, and a fertilizer high in potassium. Container-grown tomatoes will need to be watered at least once a day. Tomatoes will grow in separate containers, or community containers, and are very suited to growing in bags: Cut several slits into the upper surface of a bag of potting soil in a container, and plant tomato plants into the slits.

HERBS

Herbs in containers have distinct advantages. They can be grown in pretty pots separately, or mixed in larger containers which become virtually a selfstanding garden.

Many of them grow willingly in hanging baskets – mint, parsley, thyme and rosemary will all take to basket planting – or in windowboxes outside a kitchen window or other window on the sunny side of the house. Even a few individual pots on the kitchen windowsill will supply a surprisingly large amount of herbs for cooking, and there is no doubt that herbs add something special to any cooking.

Most herbs have interesting leaf forms in addition to being aromatic, and can be used as foliage with flowering plants. Flowering herbs should also be included in any container-grown collection of fragrant plants.

Multi-storey containers, such as strawberry pots, are ideal for growing various herbs in a confined space.

If you have a large container, buy a selection of herbs in plastic bags, plant them, bags and all, into the container, and surround them with compost, potting mix or garden soil. They will then be contained, and not be tempted to send their roots far and wide.

Growing conditions

Many herbs come from a hot dry climate, but they nevertheless need food and water. Most prefer a place in the sun, although parsley, mint and sweet violets will grow in the shade.

Planting and routine care

When planting several different herbs in the same container, make sure that the more vigorous ones, such as mint, do not overwhelm slower-growing varieties.

As herbs are regularly picked, they need a good, rich soil and regular watering to help them produce a continuous supply of leaves and stems. They also need adequate nutrients in the form of liquid manure or general fertilizer to replenish the soil. If the foliage is greatly diminished by picking, give the plant a teaspoon of 2:3:2 followed by a good drenching.

On a more delicate note, as many herbs are used in their raw state, containers should be kept out of reach of dogs.

Most herbs will grow well in containers for many years, provided that their general growing conditions are favourable. With their large variety of leaf shapes and colours, herbs should not be regarded as purely utilitarian, but can be used to create very attractive planting schemes.

Far left: Economy of space results from suspending baskets of herbs in hanging baskets from three poles.

Left: Borage, leeks, lavender, rosemary, lemon grass, lettuce, nasturtiums and strawberries happily grow together in a formal herb garden incorporating several containers.

• *Herbs for Containers* •

Basils *(Ocimum basilicum)* are many and varied, and all of them attractive and useful as garnishes and in cooking. They have pretty leaves, from dark burgundy to gold, and make attractive foliage companions in mixed containers. They need rich, well-drained soil, full sun, and plenty of water when growing. Keep pinching out the growing tips to encourage dense, bushy growth.

Bay tree *(Laurus nobilis)* grows well in a pot, and can be clipped into shape (which makes it suitable for topiary). It will need daily watering in hot dry weather. Give it a fertilizer high in nitrogen, and in winter, cut down on the water. In very cold parts, move it into a sheltered position in winter (*see also* p. 70).

Chamomile *(Chamaemelum nobile)*, usually sold by nurseries as *Anthemis nobilis*, has pretty paper-like flowers, and can be grown on its own, or with other herbs such as lemon balm and parsley. The feathery leaves of chamomile are decorative and will make their own statement as foliage with several plants grown together. The flowers are used for tea and medicinal purposes.

Chives *(Allium schoenoprasum)* have attractive foliage and pretty mauve flowers, and have many uses as a garnish and in cooking. They look good when planted in an attractive pot, or they will mix readily with other herbs and vegetables, acting as an insect deterrent. Flowering chives make a pretty edging, but remove the flowers if you want to grow them primarily for culinary use to prevent the plants becoming exhausted. The pretty white flowers of garlic chives *(A. neapolitanum, see* p. 52) have a sweet scent and make a pretty sight in a mixed container.

Dill *(Anethum graveolens)* is attractive enough to grow purely as a decorative plant with its feathery dark green leaves and starry clusters of yellow-green flowers which provide seeds used in pickling. Their soil should not be over-rich, and they need full sun. Dill can take on an untidy look, and self-sewn seeds may become a problem in a mixed container.

Lavender *(Lavandula spp.)* is one of the most attractive and fragrant of all herbs. The popular and hardy French lavender *(L. stoechas)* carries its fragrance in its small, blue flowers, while English lavender *(L. angustifolia)* has aromatic, grey-green foliage which contrasts beautifully with green foliage plants. Lavender also makes an excellent companion for roses. These rewarding plants are easy to grow and undemanding, and thrive in full sun.

Lavender combines well with other plants and is a popular choice for containers as it is both decorative and has a lovely fragrance. Here it has been planted with felicia and verbenas.

Lemon balm *(Melissa officinalis)* has full, aromatic foliage which needs good, rich soil and plenty of water to keep it going. The lemon scent of its bright green leaves is released when the leaves are brushed against. Chopped leaves are used in salads. The variegated varieties are the best choice for planting around the edge of a mixed container.

Mint *(Mentha spp.)* will grow in shade, semi-shade or full sun, and is better planted on its own, or confined to its own bag or container, as it has the habit of spreading far and wide in no time at all. Keep it well clipped for a bushy growth. Spearmint *(M. spicata)* is probably the most popular for culinary use, while variegated applemint *(M. suaveolens)* looks particularly attractive tumbling over the edge of a container or the side of a hanging basket.

Nasturtium *(Tropaeolum majus)* is often treated as part of the herb garden, as in addition to brightening up the garden, both its flowers and its leaves are edible. It needs full sun and ordinary soil, and not a great deal of water (*see also* p. 46).

Oregano *(Origanum vulgare)*, also known as wild marjoram, is an invaluable culinary herb and a highly decorative plant which will grow into a compact cushion of leaves. Its pink flowers are attractive, which makes it ideal as an edging plant in a large container. It needs full sun and ordinary soil. Older plants may become woody and untidy after about three years, when they should be divided and replanted.

Parsley *(Petroselinum crispum)*, one of the most attractive and best known herbs with its tightly curled leaves, looks good on its own, or may be used as an edging plant in a mixed container. *P. crispum* var. *neopolitanum* (plain-leafed parsley) is less attractive, but has a stronger flavour which some people prefer for culinary use. Parsley needs good soil and prefers semi-shade, but will also grow in full sun. Do not allow it to flower. Seeds take a long time to germinate, so it may be better to buy seedlings.

Rosemary *(Rosmarinus officinalis)* is such a widely used culinary herb, that no container-grown herb garden should be without it. With its small, evergreen, grey-green leaves and spikes of small flowers varying from dark to pale blue and white, it is worth planting this hardy shrub purely for ornamental purposes. Dwarf rosemary *(R. lavandulaceus)* is a lovely, fragrant groundcover. Plant rosemary in full sun or partial shade, in light, well-drained soil.

Sage *(Salvia officinalis)* is one of the most ornamental herbs, especially the variegated varieties. They have their own distinctive flavour, and, being of Mediterranean origin, need full sun, soil which is not over-rich, and regular picking.

Salad burnet *(Poterium sanguisorba)* is used only as a garnish and added to salads for its crisp cucumber taste. It thrives in full sun and its long, cascading stems can be straggling and untidy, so keep the plants clipped back when young. Flower heads should be removed regularly to prevent self-sown seedlings from becoming a problem.

Sweet marjoram *(Origanum majorana)* makes an attractive container plant with its trailing stems and clusters of dainty pink, white or purple flowers. It needs full sun and fertile soil, and is frost tender.

Sweet violets *(Viola odorata)* and heartsease *(V. tricolor)* were once widely used for the healing of wounds, but nowadays they are used more as a decorative adjunct to the herb garden, although they make a lovely garnish. They are good mixers, and heartsease will cascade over the edge of a mixed planting. They thrive in partial shade in moist, fertile soil.

Thymes *(Thymus spp.)* are highly aromatic plants with various scents, including lemon, and have an attractive growth, some of them with variegated leaves. There are good decorative and flowering varieties for containers and several different thymes in a windowbox could look particularly attractive. They need full sun, and ordinary soil, and need to be clipped back regularly to prevent them from becoming untidy and straggly. Give them very well-drained soil, and only use organic compost as they will not tolerate chemical fertilizer.

A colourful variety of lettuces and dainty violas make a pretty picture and a welcome addition to the kitchen garden.

· Fruit for Containers ·

Although the variety of fruit suitable for container-planting may not be great, certain types of fruit do exceptionally well in containers.

Calamondin *(Citrus mitis). See* p. 70.

Cape gooseberries *(Physalis peruviana)* are easy to grow and thrive under warm, sub-tropical conditions. The berries are lovely eaten fresh, or used in jams and pies. Good drainage is essential, as is regular watering. Reduce water after the active growing season to encourage fruit development. Plant this perennial in its own half-barrel or tub, and prune hard after fruiting.

Chinese guava *(Psidium cattleianum).* This smaller, slow-growing species of guava will take well to being planted in a large pot. It bears a good crop of small, round, red fruit from late winter to early spring and will tolerate moderate frost. It needs little pruning, and pinching out the growing tip to promote bushy growth will usually suffice.

Kumquats *(Fortunella japonica). See* p. 75.

Lemon trees *(Citrus limon).* Both lemons and limes *(C. aurantifolia)* are among the citrus trees that grow well in containers. These evergreen trees bear fruit for most of the year and look attractive all year round. Plant them in well-drained soil in a good-sized pot, and give them a sunny, sheltered position. Although they will tolerate cool conditions, they are sensitive to frost.

Passion fruit *(Passiflora edulis)* can grow up a trellis or be trained over a pergola in warmer areas with mild winters, on the north side of the house. This climber, also known as granadilla, needs well-drained soil and warm, moist conditions to thrive. It is a rampant grower and needs to be constantly clipped back to keep it in check, especially if grown on a balcony.

Strawberries *(Fragaria spp.)* can be planted in strawberry pots, tubs or barrels and are attractive when flowering and fruiting. They thrive in slightly acid, well-composted, well-drained soil. They need frequent watering and protection from excessive heat in summer. Good mulching helps to keep the plants moist, and the fruit clean. Combine strawberries with flowering annuals such as pansies and primulas.

Opposite: Nasturtium (tropaeolum), valued for its leaves and seeds, makes a colourful addition to any herb garden. Below: A calamondin with variegated leaves is attractive all year round.

Yellow alyssum creates a golden cascade from an old tree stump. Opposite: A fringe of ivy has been given to the small bird-bath with its bronze statue directing the flow of water.

CHAPTER 9

Plant Care and Maintenance

Keeping a plant in a container is rather like keeping an animal in a cage – a container plant is almost completely reliant on you for its wellbeing. The plants in our gardens come from all parts of the world, where many types of soil and climate exist, and knowing a little about their natural habitat helps greatly in determining their needs. A plant that originates from a sub-tropical area is not likely to do well in a part of the country where winters are long and frosty. The basic requirements of any plant are water, food, light, warmth, air, and a means of support (usually soil). Special attention to all these requirements is particularly necessary for contained plants which cannot send their roots out in search of food and water.

The mauve scaevola in a moulded container does well on a sunny patio.

Soil

Soil lends support to the plant, and it is through the soil that the roots find their way to water and food. Only food which has dissolved in water is available to those countless, infinitely fine root hairs that arise from the main roots of the plant. These same roots need air in order to carry out their crucial duties – under waterlogged conditions, the fine roots will soon rot and die. For this reason good drainage in the soil is essential to allow surplus water to drain away.

Plants grown in containers have a limited amount of soil, and it is therefore very important to start off with good soil and then pay special attention to regular feeding and watering. Most gardeners have their own special recipe for their

container plants, but the following ingredients will give a good general mix:

- Four parts good, rich, loose garden soil
- Two parts leafmould, slightly ground
- Two parts coarse, clean sand
- One part kraal manure, well rotted

To every 25 litres of soil, add half a cup of bone meal and one tablespoon of superphosphates, or 2:3:2, or slow-release fertilizer such as *Osmocote*. Mix well before use. The addition of charcoal will keep the soil sweet. Use large pieces to improve drainage, and mix smaller pieces with the soil. For those plants which simply must have the best possible drainage, such as bromeliads and most ferns, the addition of pine bark chips or small stones will also help.

Special requirements

Many different soil mixes are available which have been specially prepared for special plants, such as ferns, African violets, hydrangeas, and acid-loving plants. Ferns, begonias and philodendrons are among those plants which will need more organics in the soil, while cacti and succulents will need more sand.

Acid-loving plants such as azaleas, rhododendrons, pieris and camellias that are not grown in acid soil, will need to have a tablespoon of ammonium sulphate sprinkled on the surface and well watered in. Do this every three months.

Soil is a living thing, and it should be kept in good condition at all times. If it becomes hard and compacted, it should be replaced, and at the beginning of the season, in early spring, a layer of new soil to the depth of at least 5 cm should be laid on the surface, after gently cultivating the existing soil.

A large hanging basket of echeveria dominates this patio, filled with well-maintained plants, their containers concealed by the rocks.

Water

As a large proportion of a plant consists of water, it will need regular supplies to keep it going. Container-grown plants, in particular, need regular watering, as they can only take in nutrients dissolved in water. But it is very easy to overwater plants in confined conditions, resulting in sour soil and damaged roots – if a plant is waterlogged, its roots cannot breathe.

There are several methods of watering a container plant. It can be watered with a can or hose, always gently so as not to disturb the soil surface. Submersion or dunking means placing the entire plant, together with its container, into water. This method is often used for watering hanging baskets which tend to dry out very quickly. This certainly makes sure that the plant is well watered but it must be carefully done. Better still is to place the container in water to a depth of 10 cm, and allowing the water to soak up into the pot.

Those gardeners who have a large number of containers in the garden often resort to having a drip-irrigation system installed, which can then be controlled. The more sophisticated systems can also have fertilizer incorporated into the water. Tree ferns, for instance, which require a great deal of water, appreciate having their own microjet system.

When to water

A good rule is to water only when the plant is dry, or almost dry, and this can be gauged by gently digging down into the soil with one's finger, to feel whether the soil is damp. In hot, windy conditions you may need to water more often, while plants will require less frequent watering in damp, cool conditions.

A good soaking once or twice a week is infinitely better than regular sprinkling on the soil surface, which will only encourage the tender roots to come up to the surface, and possibly be burned. In very warm weather, hanging baskets may need watering twice a day, in the early morning and early afternoon.

Special containers

On the market today are several types of container which are self-watering, that is, a supply of water is placed in the base of the pot, or in a reservoir, and is made available as the plant needs it. This type is useful on that part of the patio which does not receive rain, but where rain reaches the plant, this system is wasted.

Many containers come complete with drip trays, which prevent surplus water from wetting the surrounding paving, but care should be taken to see that this is not constantly full of water.

Additional requirements

The shiny leaves of philodendrons, syngoniums and ivies can be sprayed with water, but the hairy leaves of stachys, cinerarias and helichrysum should not be sprayed. Misting is recommended for fuchsias, azaleas and camellias.

In some parts of South Africa, the water is highly alkaline, and it may be necessary to adjust this by the addition of ammonium sulphate or some other acid agent. Yellowing of plants' leaves may be a sign of highly alkaline water.

Ferns and other plants which need a high humidity, can suffer on hot, dry days, but if they are placed on a layer of pebbles, with water just covering the pebbles, the plants will benefit greatly from the added moisture in the air.

NUTRIENTS

This is a difficult subject indeed, as the needs of plants are so many and varied. Generally, plants will need more food from spring through summer, when most plants are growing. Cut down when the colder weather comes. However, winter and spring flowering annuals and bulbs will need extra food during autumn and winter. Nutrients generally need to be replaced more frequently for container-grown plants.

Plants should only be fertilized when they are in good growth. After repotting, plants should be allowed to settle down before applying more fertilizer. Always water plants thoroughly after any application of fertilizer to prevent fertilizer burn.

Forms of nutrients

Food may be in the form of chemical fertilizer, containing varying proportions of nitrogen, phosphates and potassium (N.P.K.). Plants valued for their leaves will need more nitrogen, whereas those which produce berries and flowers will need more potassium.

Organic food not only feeds the plant, but improves the texture of the soil. It may be animal, such as kraal or poultry which must be well rotted, or it may be plant material such as leafmould or compost.

Compost is regarded as black gold, with its ability to bring sustenance to the soil.

Another form of food is liquid manure, which is very useful as it gets right down to the roots where it is needed. Liquid manure may be made of poultry manure, or may be derived from seaweed and fish emulsion, the latter two being highly nutritious.

Foliar feeding involves spraying the leaves with a diluted liquid fertilizer containing vitamins and trace elements absorbed directly through the leaves. Make sure that the fertilizer is well diluted to prevent damage to tender leaves, and never use more fertilizer than the quantity stipulated on the container. With the ever-growing popularity of container plants, attention has been given to the production of food for special plants, such as roses, azaleas and citrus, and it is certainly well worthwhile investing in these, particularly because they are well balanced.

LIGHT

Direct sunlight, good light but not direct sun, shade and semi-shade, are conditions which vary with different plants, and can make a great deal of difference to their appearance and perfor-

The pale leaves of variegated hibiscus will lighten a shady area. Hibiscus will not tolerate heavy frost.

mance. Adverse effects can be burning of leaves and flowers in too strong sunshine, or yellowing of leaves in too deep shade.

Plants are wonderfully adapted to finding their way to the light of the sun, which is life-giving, but if they are placed in too shady conditions, they can take on a wan, straggling appearance in their efforts to reach the sun. Therefore, knowing the shade and light needs of a plant is important. This information can be obtained by determining its original habitat – whether it comes from a humid jungle where it grows in deep shade, or from the desert where it is used to maximum exposure to the sun.

During hot, dry weather, container plants as well as their surroundings should be sprayed to keep them cool and damp.

Generally, plants with dark green leaves will survive in deeper shade. The aspidistra (see p. 59) is a fine example of this, being able to survive in dense shade, and most ferns prefer the shade. On the other hand, plants with coloured leaves, such as coleus or codiaeums (crotons) will need much more light, and desert dwellers can tolerate the sun all day. Annual flowering plants, on the whole, will need full sun, whereas many perennials, including epiphyllums, zygocactus, fuchsias and streptocarpus will willingly flower in the shade.

Trees for shade

Light does not necessarily mean sunlight. Many plants will grow only where the light is good, but will not tolerate direct sun, which may burn the plants. In the garden, trees will bring welcome shade. If the tree's growth is sparse and delicate, it will produce dappled shade, ideal for many container-grown plants, but where the foliage of the tree is dense, the shade may be too intense for the growing of plants. However, if the lower branches of the tree are removed, this will make available good, strong light. Take off a few branches at a time, making sure you keep the tree to a good shape.

Deciduous trees have the advantage of letting in the sun during winter when their branches are bare of leaves, enabling you to place pots of flowering winter and spring bulbs and annuals under them. Then, as the leaves come to the branches, containers filled with shade lovers can be brought back.

Placing of containers

In South Africa, the sun apparently moves north in winter, bringing warmth to a north-facing patio or wall, then in summer, the sun comes south, but at all times of the year, a south-facing wall or garden will be in shade. This will influence the placing of containers of plants whose shade requirements differ. Camellias, for instance, can be placed at the edge of the shade on the south side of a tree, where it will receive good light all through summer, when its leaves are growing and the buds forming. Then, when it comes into flower, in winter, the blooms will be protected from the full sun, as the sun goes north, creating shade on the south side.

AIR

All plants need a good movement of air around them, but none of them like a draught, which often occurs on a patio where plants are placed near a door. Wind may damage leaves and flowers, and cause a loss of moisture, and plants which are prone to this need a sheltered position. Plants with large leaves, such as philodendrons, are easily damaged by wind through tearing, and, if the wind is constant, this causes burning of the leaves, depicted by browning of their margins. Draughts and wind can be kept at bay through the use of a trellis, or plants which are virtually unaffected, such as conifers whose fine leaves can withstand the wind.

Repotting

A plant should never be placed in a pot which is too large for it, as the nutrients in a vast amount of soil will not be taken up. Rather allow a plant to sit comfortably in its container, with a few centimetres to spare all round, and repot it when it grows too big for the container.

Generally, after two or more years in a container, plants may become rootbound and need fresh soil. Symptoms that a plant needs repotting are: there is not much new healthy growth; roots are growing through the drainage holes; roots have filled the pot to such an extent that it is difficult to water it; the soil is hard and compacted.

Deciduous trees can be removed completely when they are dormant, have their roots trimmed, then planted back into their containers which have been replenished.

Preparing the container

The new container should be only one, or, at the most two, sizes larger than the existing one. Cleanliness and hygiene must be maintained at all times. Always scrub out a container after use before refilling and planting it up with new plants or repotting, to get rid of any pests and diseases from previous plants or soil. New containers must also be thoroughly cleaned before use to get rid of harmful salts that may be present on the surface of the container.

A good soaking of porous containers will keep them hydrated to ensure that they will not absorb the moisture from the soil which is required by the plants. Examine wooden containers for rot and remove all traces before re-use. Soak crusted containers in water to remove all traces of dirt before re-use.

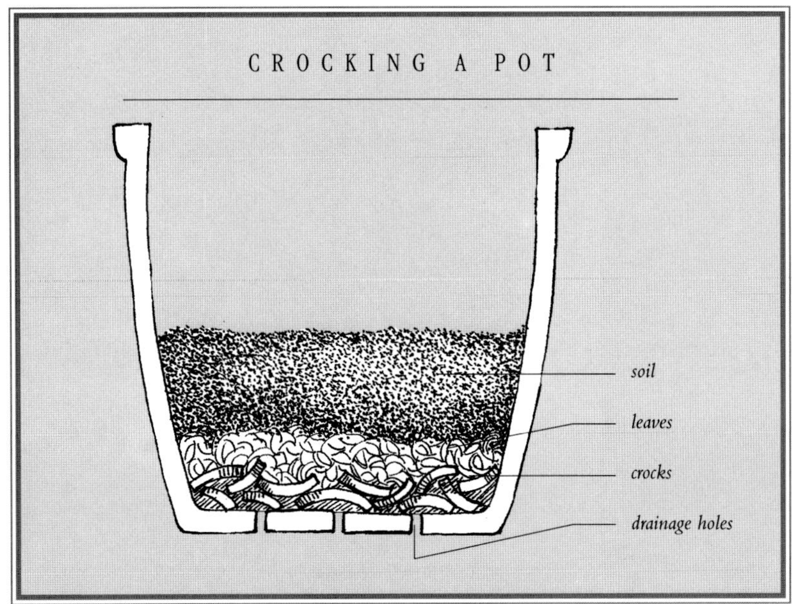

Make sure that there are sufficient drainage holes in the base of the container, and cover these with crocks or stones, followed by a layer of leaves, then the fresh soil mix. If possible, place large containers in position before adding the soil and planting them up as they may be too heavy to move once filled.

Preparing the plants

Water the plant very well before taking it out. This will facilitate removal and prevent the root ball from breaking apart or sticking to the container. If the foliage is heavy, it might be advisable to cut this back before lifting the plant, so as not to place the plant under stress.

Now lift the plant and examine the roots. If they are badly twisted, gently untangle them, and cleanly cut through the outer parts. Any damaged roots should also be removed. If the roots are tightly compacted, score them lightly with a sharp knife and gently loosen them with your fingers to stimulate new growth outward into the new soil before placing the plant into the prepared container.

Once compacted roots have been dealt with, position the plant at the same depth as previously, and water it well. If it sinks, adjust the level by adding more soil, and water again, always leaving at least 2,5 cm free above the soil level.

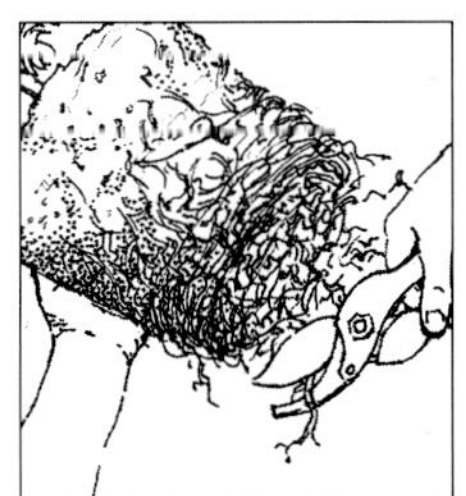

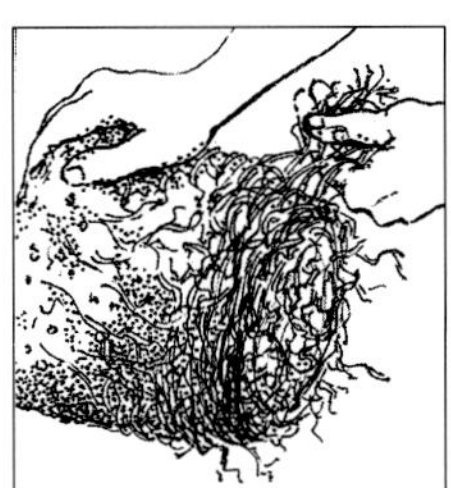

Dealing with compacted roots

TRIMMING THE ROOTS

Plants with vigorous root systems can be kept in good health between repottings by simply trimming the roots and replenishing the soil without removing the plant from its container.

Take a long, sharp knife, and cut down through the soil between the plant and the edge of the container, between 5 and 10 cm from the edge, depending on the size of the container.

Now remove all the roots and soil in that space, and replace it with well-rotted compost.

Water the plant well, and in a very short time the roots will find their way into this new source of food.

Pests and Diseases

Pests and diseases that attack container plants may be in the form of insects or fungi, and only through constantly inspecting your plants will their good health be ensured.

Caterpillars, grasshoppers, beetles and crickets are the worst insect pests, and can easily be removed by hand and destroyed.

Snails, too, can be a menace, and will have to be removed and destroyed, or a suitable snail bait can be laid down. Most snail baits are highly poisonous, and should only be used if they can be placed out of reach of birds, pets and children. A safer remedy would be to place saucers of beer or wine inside the containers, where the snails will happily drown.

One grower of hostas always applies a good, thick layer of vaseline around the lip of each container, which, she swears, keeps the snails away from her plants.

The rhino beetle is the worst pest of all for container-grown palms. It penetrates and destroys the growing tip of the palm, killing the plant. The first signs of its presence are small piles of loose plant material excavated by the beetle, and if it is extracted immediately, it may not be too late to save the plant.

Scale can come with a change in the weather, and can be lightly dabbed with methylated spirits, as can mealybugs.

Aphids, if noticed early enough, can be gently removed by hand. If they persist, sprinkle insect powder around the main stem of the plant.

Spider mites, or red spider, exists on the underside of plants' leaves in the from of a series of fine webs and tiny orange spots.

Quite often, thorough watering of the underside of the leaves will deal with this problem. If this does not rid you plants of the spider mites, try an insecticide applied locally.

Mealybug is a common pest, especially among palms. Affected leaves can be painted with a solution of equal parts of milk and methylated spirits, or, if the infestation is great, spray the affected plants with *Karbaspray*.

Karbaspray will also deal with red spider mite, but before resorting to this, try spraying the undersides of the affected leaves with a strong jet of water. This will obviously depend on the placing of your containers.

Fungus diseases such as mildew and wilt may be more prevalent in container plants on the patio than those in the garden, possibly owing to poor air circulation. As soon as they occur, they should be treated immediately with a good fungicide, and any damaged tissue should be removed and destroyed.

Root rot sometimes occurs in newly planted annual seedlings. The entire plant, together with the surrounding soil, should be discarded.

Propagation

Most gardeners enjoy the challenge of producing more plants from their own special specimens. The main methods of propagation are as follows:

Leaves

Many plants can be propagated by cutting through the heavy veins on the underside of their leaves, then laying the leaves down onto moist soil. Young plants will soon arise from these cuts. Some plants propagated in this way are African violets and begonias. Most succulents can be propagated by placing their leaves upright in moist sand. New plants will arise from the base.

Suckers

Some plants send out suckers, from the ends of which new plants will develop, for example *Nandina domestica* (heavenly bamboo). These new, young plants can be cleanly cut away and planted into their own pots.

Cuttings

Cuttings can be taken either from the season's mature growth, from new spring growth, or from plants which are dormant. All cuttings should be taken from healthy plants. Tip cuttings of about 10 cm are taken from new spring growth. Leave the top two to four leaves, trim each leaf to half the size, then remove all the other leaves before planting.

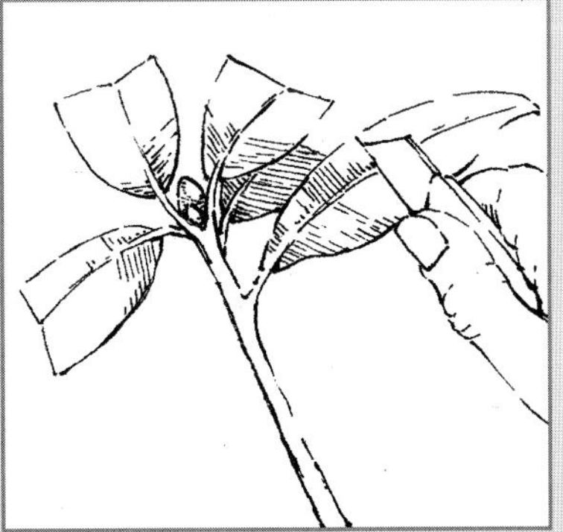

Cuttings of mature growth are usually taken in summer, of shrubs such as azaleas. Cuttings of deciduous plants, taken when they are dormant, can be up to 25 cm long, and planted at two thirds their depth. Hormone powders are useful for encouraging new roots to form, and the soil or growing medium should be well drained.

LAYERING

Take a section from the mother plant, make a shallow cut on the underside and place this section, cut down, into a new pot. When a good root system has developed, the new plant can be cut away from the mother plant. Clematis is highly successful when propagated in this manner.

Seeds

This is the most economical means of gaining new plants, as a small pinch of seeds will bring a lot of new plants. They can be sown into trays, or sown straight into the containers. Scatter seeds of annuals around bulbs planted into pots.

WINTER COLD AND DORMANCY

Deciduous shrubs and trees, having lost their leaves in autumn, will need a good winter rest, and should be given the minimum of water during their dormant period.

Bulbs and bulbous plants, such as hippeastrum, tuberous begonias and gloxinias, will die down in autumn, and their pots can then be moved to a sheltered place where they can stay until spring. In spring, new growth can be encouraged by watering, taking care that drainage is good. As the new growth becomes stronger, special potplant food can be applied to the gently scarified soil, with a layer of compost laid on the surface, followed by a good soaking. If the plant has become too big for its pot, this is the time to repot it (*see* p. 121).

Liliums will die down after flowering, often in mid-summer, and the containers can then be moved to a cool, dry place. In summer rainfall areas, if it is not possible to move the container, cover it with hessian or shade cloth to prevent heavy rain from reaching the bulbs, as too much water could damage them.

Protect plants which cannot take heavy frost, and whose containers are too large to move, with a wigwam of hay or straw. Alternatively, hessian can be wrapped around four sticks placed in the pot. Never use plastic for this purpose, as any parts of the plant touching it could be burnt.

MOVING CONTAINERS

Generally, containers should be moved as little as possible once planted, to avoid damage to both plants and containers. But sometimes containers have to be moved to fit in with a change in your garden design, or because certain plants need a more sheltered position.

There are special trolleys available for moving containers, consisting of a platform with casters at each corner. Many nurseries have special low-based trolleys available for moving containers – try hiring one of these.

If you have a rotor mower which is of no use, remove the motor and other structures, leaving only the handle, the four wheels and the metal base. This will make a very good container mover. You could also use a board mounted on lengths of metal pipe to act as rollers, or place the container on strong sacking or cardboard and drag it to its new position.

Never water plants before moving their containers, as this will add a lot of extra weight. Trees and shrubs in containers that are being moved should be protected by tying their branches with rope or soft netting.

Special Tools

Certain special tools are essential to facilitate the task of keeping your container-grown plants in peak condition.

Watering can. This can be of metal or plastic, and it is advisable to buy one which has a spout long enough to reach the centre of large pots. A detachable rose is essential, as it is easily clogged by liquid manure.

Hand trowel. This is used for lifting and transplanting small plants and seedlings, and working in a confined space such as a container.

Hand fork. This is very useful for loosening the soil around plants, and for light digging or weeding in containers.

Hand cultivator. Use this for weeding in larger containers, and to loosen crusted soil.

Secateurs. A good pair of secateurs is essential for keeping container plants in shape.

Scissors. A pair of small, sharp scissors can be very useful for deadheading small flowers. It is also useful for cutting through leaf stems or other small stems, or for cutting herbs for use.

Pruning

The rules of pruning apply to container plants as much as they do to plants growing naturally in the garden. Any old, dead, weak or straggling growth should be removed completely all through the year. Container-grown plants are also pruned to form them into an attractive shape, to improve their growth by letting in air and light around their centre, or to encourage new growth and the development of flowers or fruit.

With many plants, to encourage bushy growth, it is sufficient to pinch out the tops of growing stems, or terminal buds (the buds growing at the end of a branch) when the plants are young.

Climbers and shrubs need routine pruning at least once a year to remove crowded, dead or crossing shoots.

Topiary plants need to be frequently clipped to keep them looking their best. Here, ivy has been encouraged to grow over a spiral of stout wire connected to a central column.

General Hints for Pruning

- Always use sharp secateurs or pruners.
- Do not leave a stub of dead wood on a plant – this could become diseased and affect the rest of the plant.
- Prune in such a way that growth is directed outwards or towards an open space, and not towards another branch.
- Try to cut a stem so that the topmost bud points outwards, allowing for good circulation in the centre of the plant.
- Remove all growth which has been pruned from around the plants.

SUCCESSIONAL PLANTING

By using successional planting of annuals and perennials with different flowering seasons and flowering periods, you can have colour in your containers all year round. To facilitate successional planting, have several plastic liners in your containers. Lift out each individual section that needs replacement after flowering, complete with its soil and plastic. Reline that section and replant with new plants. By regularly relining and replanting the individual sections you can ensure a lasting display of colour without having to replant the entire container.

Separate plastic bags filled with potting soil and flowering plants and placed in a container with compost around and on top of the bags to hide the bags will also work. Water carefully to ensure that the water reaches the plants and does not go to waste between the bags. Remove and replace the bags as the flowers die down.

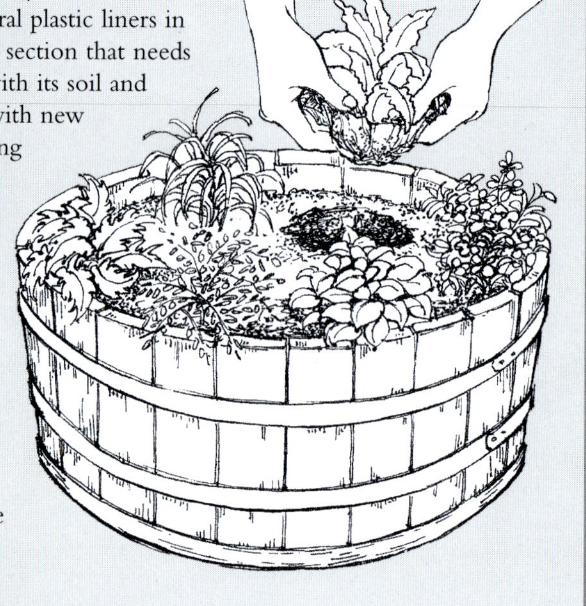

Chrysanthemums bought ready-potted should be regularly watered to keep them growing and, after flowering, can be planted out into the garden.

Deciduous climbers, trees and shrubs are normally pruned in autumn, while evergreens are pruned before they start making new shoots in spring. Shrubs and climbers flowering in spring and early summer are best pruned after the flowering period.

With many plants there is no specific pruning time – simply remove dead or weak stems when you see them. *Clematis montana* is best left unpruned, apart from removing very dense growth. Clematis hybrids are cut back almost to ground level in autumn.

In Conclusion

Plants in containers need more special care than those in the ground, but this does not mean that they are more difficult to grow.

Seeing to their comfort is a worthwhile task, which will result in plants which are attractive, in glowing good health, and a real asset to their surroundings.

Index